YOGA VEDANTA SUTRAS

YOGA VEDANTA SUTRAS

Sri Swami Sivananda

Published by

THE DIVINE LIFE SOCIETY

P.O. SHIVANANDANAGAR—249 192

Distt. Tehri-Garhwal, Uttaranchal, Himalayas, India

Price]   **2006**   [**Rs. 60/-**

Part I—First Edition: 1955
Part II—First Edition: 1958
Part I & II—First Edition: 2006

[1,000 Copies]

ISBN 81-7052-185-8

ES 87

Published by Swami Vimalananda for
The Divine Life Society, Shivanandanagar, and printed by him at
the Yoga-Vedanta Forest Academy Press,
P.O. Shivanandanagar, Distt. Tehri-Garhwal, Uttaranchal,
Himalayas, India

SRI SWAMI SIVANANDA

SRI SWAMI SIVANANDA

Born on the 8th September, 1887, in the illustrious family of Sage Appayya Dikshitar and several other renowned saints and savants, Sri Swami Sivananda had a natural flair for a life devoted to the study and practice of Vedanta. Added to this was an inborn eagerness to serve all and an innate feeling of unity with all mankind.

His passion for service drew him to the medical career; and soon he gravitated to where he thought that his service was most needed. Malaya claimed him. He had earlier been editing a health journal and wrote extensively on health problems. He discovered that people needed right knowledge most of all; dissemination of that knowledge he espoused as his own mission.

It was divine dispensation and the blessing of God upon mankind that the doctor of body and mind renounced his career and took to a life of renunciation to qualify for ministering to the soul of man. He settled down at Rishikesh in 1924, practised intense austerities and shone as a great Yogi, saint, sage and Jivanmukta.

In 1932 Swami Sivananda started the Sivanandashram. In 1936 was born The Divine Life Society. In 1948 the Yoga-Vedanta Forest Academy was organised. Dissemination of spiritual knowledge and training of people in Yoga and Vedanta were their aim and object. In 1950 Swamiji undertook a lightning tour of India and Ceylon. In 1953 Swamiji convened a 'World Parliament of Religions'. Swamiji is the author of over 300 volumes and has disciples all over the world, belonging to all nationalities, religions and creeds. To read Swamiji's works is to drink at the Fountain of Wisdom Supreme. On 14th July, 1963 Swamiji entered Mahasamadhi.

GURU STOTRAS

(The Sadhaka is requested to repeat these Guru Stotras, before taking up the daily study of these Sutras. This wholesome practice will not only earn for him the grace and blessings of the Brahma-Vidya Gurus, but create in him the proper frame of mind to absorb the Truths revealed in these Sutras.)

गुरुर्ब्रह्मा   गुरुर्विष्णुर्गुरुर्देवो   महेश्वरः ।
गुरुः साक्षात् परं ब्रह्म तस्मै श्रीगुरवे नमः ॥

अज्ञानतिमिरान्धस्य   ज्ञानाञ्जनशलाकया ।
चक्षुरुन्मीलितं येन तस्मै श्रीगुरवे नमः ॥

अखण्डमण्डलाकारं व्याप्तं येन चराचरम् ।
तत्पदं दर्शितं येन तस्मै श्रीगुरवे नमः ॥

चैतन्यं शाश्वतं शान्तं व्योमातीतं निरञ्जनम् ।
नादबिन्दुकलातीतं तस्मै श्रीगुरवे नमः ॥

ध्यानमूलं गुरोर्मूर्तिः पूजामूलं गुरोः पदम् ।
मन्त्रमूलं गुरोर्वाक्यं मोक्षमूलं गुरोः कृपा ॥

ब्रह्मानन्दं परमसुखदं केवलं ज्ञानमूर्तिं
द्वन्द्वातीतं गगनसदृशं तत्त्वमस्यादिलक्ष्यम् ।
एकं नित्यं विमलमचलं सर्वधीसाक्षिभूतं
भावातीतं त्रिगुणरहितं सद्गुरुं तं नमामि ॥

THE SUPREME POWER OF GOD'S NAME

हरे राम हरे राम राम राम हरे हरे ।
हरे कृष्ण हरे कृष्ण कृष्ण कृष्ण हरे हरे ॥

"The MAHAMANTRA is an all-powerful mysterious Divine Power." — *Swami Sivananda.*

The Divine Name is verily the seed and origin of the entire Universe. God's Name is the Supreme Redeemer. Name is the ultimate refuge of all creatures and the Guiding power for the world.

There is verily no greater meditation or Japa than the practice of the Divine Name. Taking recourse to the Name is equal to the highest renunciation. Name is the royal road to perfection. There is no merit (Punya) more superior to the merit of repeating the Divine Name. Practice of the Name is equal to the highest austerity.

Name is the supreme Dharma. It is your spiritual light and guide and friend. O Man! The Name of God is your very life. Know it to be the greatest wealth of wealths. Name is the one Great Reality in this false show of fleeting, perishable forms. It is indeed the dearest and the sweetest thing in this world. Nama is the permanent Truth behind all these passing appearances.

If you repeat God's Name either with faith or even in fun, the most auspicious Name will illumine your entire being and fill you with bliss and peace. There is no doubt about this. In whatsoever manner you utter the Divine Name of the Lord you will be freed from all delusion of Maya and will attain the Supreme Blessedness from which there is no more any return to pain and sorrow. You will abide in eternal bliss and Light.

मधुरं मधुरेभ्योऽपि मङ्गलेभ्योऽपि मङ्गलम् ।
पावनं पावनेभ्योऽपि हरेर्नामैव केवलम् ॥१ ॥

If there is anything sweeter than all sweet things, more auspicious than all auspicious objects and more purifying than all purifying agencies, it is the NAME OF HARI AND HARI ALONE.

आब्रह्मस्तम्बपर्यन्तं सर्वं मायामयं जगत् ।
सत्यं सत्यं पुनः सत्यं हरेर्नामैव केवलम् ॥२ ॥

The whole creation from Brahma down to the meanest blade of grass is illusory. If there is anything real, it is the NAME OF HARI AND HARI ALONE, which is thrice true.

स गुरुः स पिता चापि स माता स च बान्धवः ।
शिक्षयेच्चेत् सदा स्मर्तुं हरेर्नामैव केवलम् ॥३ ॥

He is a teacher, father, mother and friend, all in one, who exhorts us to remember constantly one thing, viz., the NAME OF HARI.

निःश्वासे न हि विश्वासः कदा रुद्धो भविष्यति ।
कीर्तनीयमती बाल्याद् हरेर्नामैव केवलम् ॥४ ॥

There is no certainty about the breath; it may stop its movement any moment. Therefore, what one should do is to chant from one's very childhood nothing but the NAME OF HARI.

MARKS OF SPIRITUAL PROGRESS

(Sri Swami Sivananda)

Peace, cheerfulness, contentment, dispassion, fearlessness, unperturbed state of mind under all conditions indicate that you are advancing in the spiritual path.

Spiritual progress is not measured by Siddhis or powers, but only by the depth of your bliss in meditation.

These are the sure tests of your spiritual progress:

Is your interest in inner spiritual activity and outer Sadhana increasing day after day?

Does spiritual life mean to your consciousness a matter of great delight, a delight far transcending the happiness that the world of vital pleasures affords you or offers you?

Has your personal awareness come to a possession of a sense of peace and strength which men who are not aspirants do not find in their everyday lives?

Do you feel certain that your power of discrimination and light of thought have been steadily growing?

Is your life being gradually led to such experiences which reveal to you the operation of a will and intelligence other than your own, the will and intelligence of the Omnipresent Lord?

Has there come into the conscious activities of your everyday life, the active function of a new delightful angle of vision, a new perspective, a strong sense of selfpossession, a steadily growing conviction of your dependence upon and intimate relation with the allpervading Divinity?

If your answers to all these questions or to any one of them are in the affirmative, be absolutely sure that you are progressing, and progressing speedily in the spiritual path.

LOVE

(Sri Swami Sivananda)

1. Love is the creative force of humanity.
2. Love alone will triumph.
3. Love is the true key to the divine life.
4. Love is the gate which faces the way to the infinite.
5. Love never claims, it ever gives.
6. Love ever suffers, never resents, never revenges.
7. Love is the living essence of the divine nature which beams full of all goodness.
8. Life is a sweet flower of which love is the honey.

CONTENTS

CONTENTS

ॐ

Sri Satguru Paramatmane Namah

YOGA VEDANTA SUTRAS

ॐ सहनाववतु सहनौभुनक्तु सहवीर्यं करवावहै ।
तेजस्विनावधीतमस्तु मा विद्विषावहै ॥
ॐ शान्ति शान्ति शान्ति:

Adhyaya One

KARMA YOGA SUTRAS

Pada 1

What Is Karma Yoga

1. Now then an exposition of the Karma Yoga.

2. Karma Yoga is the Yoga of selfless action without agency and expectation of fruits.

3. Work is worship of the Lord.

Fruits of Karma Yoga

4. Karma Yoga removes the impurities of the mind.

5. Karma Yoga prepares the mind for the reception of Divine Light, Divine Grace and Divine Knowledge.

6. Service of humanity is service of God.

7. Work elevates when done in the right spirit and without attachment or egoism.

8. Karma Yoga expands the heart, breaks all barriers that stand in the way of realising the ultimate unity and takes you to the door of intuition.

9. Karma Yoga helps you to develop divine virtues such as mercy, tolerance, kindness, cosmic love, patience, self-restraint, etc.

10. Karma Yoga destroys jealousy, hatred, malice, and the idea of superiority.

11. There is indescribable joy in the practice of Karma Yoga.

Bhava in Karma Yoga

12. The Bhakta has Nimitta Bhava.

13. He feels: "I am an instrument in the hands of the Lord. God does everything."

14. My body, mind and senses and everything belong to the Lord alone.

15. A student of Vedanta cultivates Sakshi Bhava.

16. He feels: "All actions are done by the qualities of Nature only. Prakriti works. I am only a witness."

17. "I am the pure actionless Atman. I am Akarta (non-doer). I am Abhokta (non-enjoyer). I am Asanga (unattached)."

18. "I am distinct from the senses, body and mind."

19. "Seeing, hearing, talking, acting, etc., all belong to the senses. They are Dharmas of the senses. I have nothing to do with them."

20. While serving others a Vedanti sees his self in others, whereas a Bhakta beholds the Lord in others.

Pada 2
Instructions to Karma Yogins

21. No work is mean to a Karma Yogi.

22. Do not make any difference between menial and respectable work.

23. Fix the mind on the Lord and give the hands to work.

24. Sing God's Name while serving others.

25. Feed the poor. Clothe the naked. Comfort the distressed.

26. Do actions as your duty — duty for duty' sake.

27. Do not expect even thanks or appreciation, applause, salute, for your work.

28. Spend one tenth of your income in charity.

29. Share what you have with others.

30. Scrutinise your inner motives always.

31. Annihilate selfish motives.

32. Give up Abhimana of all sorts. Vairagya-Abhimana, Seva-Abhimana, Tyaga-Abhimana.

33. Never feel, "I have helped that man." Always think, "The Lord has given me an opportunity to serve Him."

34. Always be on the lookout for opportunities to serve. Never miss even a single opportunity.

35. Do not be attached to the work. You must be able to give it up at any moment.

36. Discipline the body and the mind again and again for fiery service.

37. Non-attachment to work does not mean indifference.

38. Selfless actions are not soulless or heartless actions.

39. Put your heart and soul joyfully in all that you do.

40. Remember always that you are serving the Lord, that your actions are expressing His will.

41. Salute with folded hands every being you come across. Say "Om Namo Narayanaya, or Om Namah Sivaya, Sri Ram, Sri Krishna."

42. Serve the poor, the sick, saints, elders and teachers.

43. Shampoo the legs and bodies of sick persons. Feel that you are touching the body of the Lord. Feel that the energy of the Lord is flowing through your hands.

Pada 3
Philosophy of Karma Yoga

44. The doctrine of Karma expounds the riddle of life and the riddle of the universe.

45. Every thought and every deed of yours generate in

you certain tendencies which will effect your life herein and hereafter.

46. If you do good actions with a selfless spirit, you will soar high into the regions of bliss and peace. As you sow, so you reap.

47. Good actions generate good thoughts.

48. Wrong actions bring in misery, pain and unhappiness.

49. Everyone of us is governed by the law of action and reaction.

50. Your present character or personality is the total result of your previous actions and thoughts.

51. Your future depends upon your present action.

52. Man moulds his own destiny.

53. Actions by themselves do not bind a person, but it is the attachment and identification in regard to work that bind a person and bring pain and misery.

54. Karma is of three kinds, viz., Sanchita or the sum-total of all our actions in the previous births, a storehouse.

55. Prarabdha is that part of our past actions that has brought about our present birth.

56. And Agami is the result of our present actions.

57. Sanchita Karma is burnt by Jnana. Prarabdha is to be experienced presently and Agami is avoided by acting 'selflessly'.

58. It is the selfish motive that binds you.

59. Actions produce Samskaras or potential impressions that coalesce together and form tendencies.

60. Tendencies develop into habits and character.

61. If the character is pure and strong, the will also will be pure and strong.

62. Good deeds produce good character. Evil deeds generate bad character.

Pada 4

Qualifications for a Karma Yogi

63. A Karma Yogi should be equanimous in all conditions.

64. He should not be elated by praise, nor should he be depressed by censure.

65. He should always be rooted inwardly in the Atman or the Self.

66. He should feel and see his own self in all alike.

67. He should treat all alike.

68. He should always serve with Atma Bhava or Narayana Bhava.

69. "Let me do my duty," should be his motto. Work for work's sake.

70. He should never accept gifts.

71. He should speak softly, sweetly, truthfully, lovingly.

72. He should adapt, adjust and accommodate in relation to all and under all circumstances.

73. He should share what he has with others.

74. He should be absolutely unselfish.

75. He should keep his senses under control.

76. He should be cheerful always.

77. He should be very social and amiable.

78. He should be simple, humble, noble, gentle.

79. He should bear insult and injury.

80. He should observe Brahmacharya.

81. Offer all actions and their fruits, body, mind and senses and soul as flowers at the Lotus Feet of the Lord as Isvara-arpana.

82. Feel that the world is a manifestation of God.

83. Feel that you are serving God in all beings.

84. Discipline the senses, mind and the body.

85. Develop alertness, decision, discrimination, discernment, forgiveness, patience, mercy, cosmic love, tolerance, equal vision.

86. Have balanced mind. Be calm, cool and serene always.

87. Combine Bhakti or Jnana with Karma Yoga.

88. Be good and do good.

89. Keep the body strong and healthy.

90. Practise Asanas, Pranayama, running, Dhanda, Bhaitaks.

91. Keep daily spiritual diary.

92. Stick to resolves.

BHAKTI YOGA SUTRAS

Pada 1

1. Now, then, we shall expound the glorious science of devotion to God.

2. The goal of life is God-realisation.

3. In God alone will you find eternal peace. everlasting bliss and immortality.

4. The grand aim of human life is to attain God.

5. It is in God alone that you have all your desires finally fulfilled and obtain supreme peace, bliss and eternal satisfaction (Nitya Tripti).

6. Make use of this precious human birth for the achievement of this supreme purpose — God-realisation.

7. Pray to the Lord to make you desireless. But, have one strong desire and let it be for attaining God-realisation.

8. Through a life of service, devotion, purification, charity, Sadhana and meditation attain the highest Self-realisation and dwell in Supreme Bliss, Paramananda.

What Is Devotion

9. Devotion is supreme love to the Lord.

10. Devotion is supreme attachment to the Lord.

11. The notion of God means an absolutely perfect being and an absolutely perfect being must have all the possible attributes, including the attribute of existence, so God must exist.

12. The existence of God cannot be proved by any

rational arguments. It is purely a question of faith and refers to the instinctive side of man.

13. The deepest craving, the deepest aspiration in man is for eternal happiness, eternal knowledge and eternal truth. Man should search for some supernatural entity which can satisfy his deepest cravings and aspirations.

14. As we explain everything within Nature by the law of cause and effect, so also the Nature as a whole must be explained. It must have some cause. This cause must be different from the effect. It must be some supernatural entity, i.e., God.

15. Nature is not a mere chance collection of events, a mere jumble of accidents, but an orderly affair. The planets move regularly in their orbits, seeds grow into trees regularly, the seasons succeed each other in order. Now nature cannot order itself. It requires the existence of an intelligent being i.e., God, who is responsible for it.

16. Everything in Nature has some purpose. It fulfils some function or other. Certainly every object by itself cannot choose a function for itself. Their different functions ought to have been planned or designated by a single intelligent Being or God.

17. You cannot explore or probe into the Leela or sportive play of God. You must accept it with faith and reverence.

Pada 2
Nature of God

18. God is Love. Love is God.

19. God is the source for this world, body, mind, Prana and senses.

20. God Gives light to mind, sun, moon and stars.

21. God is your only Redeemer, Refuge.

22. God is your real father, mother, Guru, friend and relative.

23. God is the only Reality.

24. God is the dispenser of fruits of actions.

25. God is the designer and architect of this universe.

26. God is immanent and transcendent.

27. God is unchanging, undecaying and imperishable.

28. God is the Supreme Goal, Beauty and Truth.

29. God is Self-luminous and Self-existent.

30. God is eternal, perfect, pure, free and all-pervading.

31. God is beginningless and endless.

32. God is without pain, sorrow, fear, passion, caste, creed, sex and colour.

33. God is the indweller of your heart.

34. God is the controller and governor of this world, body and mind.

35. God is the centre of the whole creation. He is the first causeless Cause.

36. That Supreme Source of life is God.

37. The Lord has become all. He permeates all. He is all in all.

38. God is the way, the source, the goal, the truth and the life.

39. God is with form and without form, like ice and steam.

40. God is your sole refuge, benefactor and supreme master.

41. God reveals Himself to you in the form in which the devotee loves Him most.

42. God cannot be comprehended but can be realised.

43. To define God is to deny God.

44. God sees without eyes, hears without ears, works without hands and tastes without tongue.

45. God is unknowable through intellect but knowable through intuition.

46. The law and the lawgiver are one. The Eternal law is God Himself.

47. God is near and far. He is nearer to the pure and sincere, but farthest to the passionate.

48. God witnesses your thoughts and actions.

49. God is your unseen guest at your every meal.

50. God is the head of your house.

51. The reality of God is His universal existence (Sat).

52. God is not responsible for the wealth of a man or the poverty of another. Everyone bears the fruits of one's Karmas.

53. God is the greatest Doctor. He is the greatest Engineer. He is the greatest Mathematician.

54. God is the enjoyer and He is the object enjoyed.

55. God is the High and He is the Low. He is the knower and He is the known.

56. God is the word spoken and He is the breath which speaks it.

57. God is the manifest and He is the unmanifest.

58. God is the Breath of all breath, Prana of all Pranas, Self of all selves.

59. He is the One Ultimate Truth, unborn, undying, ever-lasting, ever-existent, subtle and devoid of pain and sorrow.

Pada 3
Philosophy of Bhakti

60. Bhakti or devotion is indispensable for attaining Jnana.

61. Jnana is the condition necessary for Bhakti to reach its fullest development in love.

62. Knowledge without devotion is as futile as devotion without knowledge.

63. Love follows from the basic oneness of all beings.

64. God is Being. World is becoming.

65. The creation of the world does not in any way affect the integrity of God.

66. The world does not stand apart from God, but is pervaded by Him.

67. Bhakti is not mere emotionalism but is the tuning of the will as well as the intellect towards the Divine.

68. The ideal devotee is a Karma Yogi as well as a Jnana Yogi.

69. Bhakti originated in knowledge, is essentially of the nature of love, and bursts forth in selfless action.

70. True love gives the highest wisdom.

71. No Jnana without devotion.

72. Para Bhakti and Jnana are one.

73. Diffused love is wisdom.

74. Concentrated wisdom is love.

75. True wisdom vibrates the heart.

76. Bhakti begins with love and Jnana with thinking and self-analysis. The end of both is the same, union with the Divine.

77. Bhakti begins with emotional dualism and culminates in monism.

78. Lover and the loved, the devotee and the object of devotion, are fused into one spiritual ecstasy.

79. All creation is the family of God.

80. This world is sustained by the power of God.

81. The deepest urge of life is to know God and to live in God.

82. God's Will is the very law which governs the universe.

83. All beings are controlled and guided by the Divine Will.

84. Life on this physical plane is a mere preparation for the Eternal life in God.

85. Though the Lord resides in all creatures and things, there is a difference in the degree of His manifestation in them.

86. In human beings the Lord is more manifest than in others.

87. Among human beings He is more or less manifest according to the degree of knowledge or consciousness that is realised.

88. He who follows the path of meditation knows his self as divine and one with God.

89. Any man or woman has equal right to follow the path of devotion.

90. The greatest sinner can practise devotion and attain God-realisation.

91. Though unborn, God takes birth as an Avatara to destroy the wicked, to protect virtue and to establish Dharma.

Pada 4

Maya

92. Maya is the Lord's illusory power.

93. God creates through Maya.

94. It is Maya that makes the one Universal Spirit appear as many, as embodied in multiple forms and delights in the same objects, the false ideas of 'I' and 'mine'.

95. Total, unreserved, self-surrender to the Lord alone will enable you to cross this Maya and attain His Lotus-Feet.

Pada 5

Bhakti Yoga Sadhana

96. Continually unfold yourself. Continually endeavour to get nearer to God.

97. The more you unfold yourself the more guidance you will receive and the more power you will manifest.

98. O man! Conquer thy craving. Conquer thy Moha (attachment). You will soon attain God-realisation.

99. In meditation the mind is turned back upon itself. The mind stops all the thought-waves.

100. Truth is love. Love is Lord. Speak truth. Cultivate pure unselfish love. Rest in truth. Rest in the Lord of Love.

101. Make your heart empty of all other things. Then alone will God enthrone Himself in your heart.

102. Equal vision is the test of God-realisation.

103. The way to God is through the heart.

104. God can be realised through faith, devotion, surrender and meditation.

105. Trust in the Lord. Surrender yourself to Him. He will bless you with peace and plenty. He will bestow upon thee all health, prosperity and success.

106. Worship the Lord, with true devotion; lead a life of purity, humility and selflessness.

107. Remember God. Take His Name always. Meditate upon Him.

108. Know the Lord to be the one Real Thing in the midst of unreal things.

109. Think often of God by day and by night. He is always near you and with you. He dwells in the chambers of your heart.

110. Cultivate the nine Modes of Bhakti.

111. Develop one of the Bhavas according to your temperament: Vatsalya, Sakhya, Madhurya, Santa, Dasya.

112. Dedicate all fruits of actions and the action itself to the Lord. This is entrance to devotion and freedom from bondage!

113. Worship the Lord continually. Live with Him. Put all your trust in Him.

114. Think of the Lord continuously. You will be with Him. You will dwell with Him.

115. Pray to God sincerely for strength and patience to bear, but not for deliverance from pain. Pain is a blessing from God. It is His mercy. It is His spiritual favour, He employs for your spiritual uplift and emancipation.

116. Be satisfied with any condition in which God places you.

117. God is nearer to you and more effectively present with you in sickness than in health. He is your unequalled, supreme, wonderful physician and surgeon.

118. Seek God within you, in your heart. Seek Him not elsewhere. Seek Him with faith.

119. Seek not God for favours. Such favours cannot bring you near to God. Cultivate Nishkama-Bhakti. Pine for His Grace and Mercy.

120. Quicken and enliven your faith in God. Let the flame of faith grow brighter and brighter daily.

121. Feel His presence everywhere.

122. Obtain His Grace through faith, devotion and total, unreserved self-surrender.

123. Cling to the Feet of the Lord.

124. Lead the Life Divine in right earnest.

125. Roll the beads, mentally repeating His Name.

126. Sing His praises.

127. Remember Him at all times.

128. Fix your mind on the Lotus-Feet of the Lord.

129. See the Lord in all objects.

130. Sing Lord's Names.

131. Meditate on His Form, first.

132. Then meditate on His all-pervading essence.

133. Withdraw the senses from their objects

134. Gaze within.

135. Concentrate on the heart.

136. Search for Him in the heart.

137. Practise Ahimsa, Satyam and Brahmacharya.

138. Say from the bottom of your heart: "I am Thine. All is Thine, My Lord, Thy Will be done."

139. Stick to Dharma.

140. Control the mind and the senses.

141. Kill egoism, lust, greed, hatred, etc.

142. Serve saints.

143. Serve your Guru; Guru and God are one.

144. Chant the Name and praises of the Lord. Sing His Glory. Meditate on His divine attributes.

145. Constantly remember the Lord and His presence. Serve and worship the Lord.

146. Cling to the Name of Lord. Practise the religion of sacrifice. Dedicate yourself to God. Walk in humility and love This is the way to God-realisation.

Pada 6

Auxiliaries to Bhakti

147. Study the lives of saints again. You will get a new inspiration. You will be elevated, renovated and transformed.

148. Japa, Kirtan, prayer, service of saints, meditation, Smaran are aids to God-realisation.

149. Shun evil company. Live in the company of saints.

150. Serve the sick and the poor.

151. Lead a simple life.

152. Cultivate divine virtues such as humility, tolerance, mercy, kindness, courage, selflessness, cosmic love, truthfulness purity or celibacy.

153. Take Sattvic food.

154. Live in Sattvic environments.

155. Keep your Puja or meditation room under lock and key, clean and pure

156. Meditate on the Lord in Brahmamuhurta.

157. Always give the best things — best food, best fruits, best clothes — to the servants, the poor and Sadhus. You will develop devotion.

158. Prostrate before everybody, even before donkeys and horses, what to speak of human beings even though they are considered untouchable by the community.

159. Develop Narayana-Bhava towards those whom you meet in your daily life. Serve all with Narayana-Bhava.

160. Be regular in your Puja of your Ishta Devata.

161. Offer whatever food you take to the Lord and take it as His Prasada.

162. Be good and do good.

163. Always be cheerful in the knowledge that God is the Protector of the universe.

164. Cultivate dispassion; plunge into intense practice. Never leave your Sadhana, your meditation, even for a day. You will attain God-realisation here and now.

Pada 7

Glory of the Lord's Name

165. Lord's Name purifies the heart.

166. Lord's Name burns all sins like fire.

167. Lords Name bestows immortality, peace, eternal bliss and prosperity.

168. Lord's Name destroys desires, cravings, attachment, egoism, fear, sorrow and delusion.

Pada 8

Fruits of Devotion

169. Spiritual experience is proportionate to spiritual fitness.

170. Within the temple of your own heart is the source of life, wisdom, bliss, peace and joy.

171. A devotee realises that God alone is and that there is nothing apart from Him or beyond Him.

172. Grace is in proportion to surrender. Greater the surrender, greater is the Grace.

173. The devotee experiences tremor of body, horripilation, choking of voice, thrills of joy, tearful eyes.

174. He experiences Viraha, extreme pain in forgetting God, in separation from God.

175. He whose life is rooted in the experience of the

Supreme develops love for all beings and becomes free from hatred for any man.

176. The Liberated Soul enters God in Moksha, just as the owner of a house enters his house.

Adhyaya Three

RAJA YOGA SUTRAS

Pada 1

1. Now then an exposition of Raja Yoga.

2. Raja Yoga is restraint of thoughts.

3. Yoga is union with the Lord or the supreme Soul.

4. Raja Yoga means King of Yoga, because it directly concerns with the mind.

Pada 2

Fruits of Yoga

5. Yoga confers immortality, eternal bliss, freedom, perfection, everlasting peace and perennial joy, good health and concentration of mind.

Pada 3

Vritti

6. A Vritti is a whirlpool in the mind-lake.

7. Chitta is the mind-stuff from where the Vrittis arise.

8. Thought is a thing. It is a dynamic force.

9. A Raja Yogi starts his Sadhana with the mind.

10. The eight limbs of Raja Yoga are Yama (self-restraint), Niyama (religious observances), Asana (posture), Pranayama (regulation of breath), Pratyahara (abstraction of the senses), Dharana (concentration), Dhyana (meditation) and Samadhi (Superconscious state).

11. Abhyasa (practice) and Vairagya are the two means to control the mind.

12. The practice should be continuous for a long time with great zeal and faith.

13. When the Vrittis are controlled the Yogi rests in his own Svaroopa or essential divine nature.

14. On other occasions he identifies himself with other Vrittis of the mind such as anger, lust, pride, greed, etc.

Pada 4

Qualifications of a Yogic student

15. The Yogic student must have faith and devotion to Guru and the Lord.

16. He must have faith in the teachings of his Guru and in Yogic scriptures.

17. He must have intense aspiration and dispassion.

18. He must be gentle, simple, humble and noble.

19. He must be free from crookedness, cunningness, double-dealing, harshness, greed and egoism.

Pada 5

Yogic Diet

20. Diet has intimate connection with the mind.

21. Mind is formed from the subtlest portion of food.

22. Purity of food leads to purity of mind.

23. The food should be light, wholesome, nutritious and Sattvic. Then alone meditation is possible.

24. Give up meat, fish, eggs, sour things, oil, chillies, garlic etc., as these are hindrances to meditation. They excite the passion. They are Tamasic.

25. Milk, barley, honey, butter, green dhal, fruits, vegetables, wheat are beneficial for a Yogic student. They are Sattvic.

26. Observe moderation in diet. Do not overload the stomach.

Pada 6

Mind and its control

27. Mind is a bundle of impressions, thoughts, desires and cravings.

28. Purify the mind by Japa, Tapas, right conduct or the practice of Yama (self-restraint) and meditation.

29. Suddha Manas or pure mind is filled with Sattva.

30. Asuddha Manas is filled with Rajas and Tamas.

31. The mind assumes the form of any object it intensely thinks.

32. Cosmic mind is the universal mind of the Lord.

33. Subconscious mind is Chitta. All impressions are imbedded here. It is the seat of memory.

34. Mind can attend only to one thing at a time.

35. Mind is the dividing wall between soul and body.

36. Mind is the commander-in-chief. The senses are the soldiers.

37. Egoism, greed, lust, pride and jealousy, are the attendants of the mind.

38. Man sees really with his mind and hears with his mind.

39. Fill the mind with divine thoughts. The impure thoughts will gradually vanish by themselves.

40. Mind is the organ of sensation and thoughts.

41. When the mind is Sattvic, calm and pure, you will get flashes of intuition.

42. Mind and Prana are interdependent. Prana is the overcoat of the mind.

43. Wherever there is Prana there is mind wherever there is mind, there is Prana.

44. Do Japa. Practise Pranayama and Pratyahara.

Control the senses. Become desireless. Concentrate. Meditate regularly. You can control the mind easily.

Pada 7
Philosophy of Om

45. Om is the word of power.

46. It is the symbol of God.

47. The whole world has come out of Om.

48. Om is the supreme refuge or support for everything.

49. Om is Infinite, Eternal, Immortal.

50. Om is a boat to cross this ocean of Samsara.

51. Repetition of Om and meditation on Om remove all obstacles in meditation and bestow immortality and eternal bliss.

Pada 8
Yama

52. Ahimsa (non-injury), Satya (truthfulness), Asteya (non-stealing), Brahmacharya (celibacy) and Aparigraha (non-covetousness) constitute Yama (self-restraint).

Pada 9
Ahimsa

53. Ahimsa is perfect harmlessness. It is positive cosmic love.

54. Ahimsa will develop the soul-force or will-power and spiritual strength.

55. If a man is established in Ahimsa, in his presence all enmities cease in others.

Pada 10
Satya

56. Thought, word and act should agree.

57. Truth alone triumphs, but not falsehood.

58. Ahimsa, Brahmacharya, justice, forgiveness, impartiality, self-control, endurance, goodness, compassion, fortitude are all forms of truth.

59. If anyone is established in truth, he will get Vak Siddhi, whatever he says will come to pass.

Pada 11
Asteya

60. Asteya is non-stealing.

61. Desire or want is the root-cause for stealing.

62. If you are established in non-stealing, all wealth will come to you.

Pada 12
Brahmacharya

63. Brahmacharya is freedom from sexual thoughts, sexual urge and the attraction of sex.

64. Brahmacharya lies at the very heart of Tapas or Yoga.

65. Not even an iota of spiritual progress is possible without Brahmacharya.

66. Japa, Kirtan, Sattvic food, enquiry, Pranayama, practice of Sirshasana, Sarvangasana will enable you to get success in Brahmacharya.

67. Practice of Brahmacharya converts the vital force into Ojas Sakti which is very favourable for meditation.

68. If one is established in Brahmacharya, he will have tremendous energy, gigantic will-power. He can move the whole world.

Pada 13

Aparigraha

69. Aparigraha is non-covetousness.

70. It removes anxiety, fear, sorrow, hatred, anger, untruthfulness, attachment, disappointment, agitation of mind, cares and worries.

71. It bestows peace, contentment and satisfaction.

72. If anyone is established in Aparigraha he will get memory of past life.

Pada 14

Niyama

73. Niyama is religious observance.

74. It consists of Saucha (purity internal and external), Santosha (contentment), Tapas (austerity), Svadhyaya (study of religious books) and Atmanivedana (self-surrender).

75. Through purity comes cheerfulness, contentment, conquest of senses and fitness for Self-realisation.

76. Contentment gives immense peace and happiness.

77. Through the practice of austerity come Siddhis.

78. Through self-surrender come Grace of the Lord and Samadhi.

Pada 15

Asana

79. Any steady and comfortable pose is Asana.

80. A steady pose gives concentration of mind.

81. Try to sit steady on one Asana for 3 hours. This will give you Asana Jaya or mastery over the pose.

82. Padma Asana, Siddha Asana, Sukha Asana, Svastika Asana are beneficial for the practice of meditation.

Pada 16

Pranayama

83. Pranayama is restraint of Prana.

84. Puraka is inhalation; Kumbhaka is retention of breath; Rechaka is exhalation.

85. Practise Pranayama in early morning on an empty stomach.

86. The different kinds of Pranayamas are Sukha Purvaka, Sitali, Sitkari, Uijayi, Bhastrika, Kapalabhati, Suryabheda, Bandha Traya, Kevala Kumbhaka.

87. Practice of Pranayama cures all diseases, awakens Kundalini and helps to control the mind.

Pada 17

Pratyahara

88. Pratyahara is withdrawal of the senses from their respective objets.

89. Pratyahara checks the outgoing tendencies of the mind.

90. Vairagya helps the practice of Pratyahara.

91. Observance of Mauna, moderation in diet, steadiness in pose, regularity in the practice of Pranayama, patience, tenacity, perseverance, celibacy, seclusion are all aids to Pratyahara.

Pada 18

Dharana

92. Dharana is concentration.

93. It is fixing the mind on an external object or an internal point or an idea.

94. Concentration is fixing the mind; meditation is allowing one idea to flow continuously.

95. Be serene. Be cheerful. Be patient. Be regular in your practice. Observe celibacy. Reduce your wants and activities. Mix little. Observe Mauna. These are aids to concentration.

96. Concentrate on Trikuta or heart.

Pada 19
Dhyana

97. Dhyana is meditation.

98. When you practise concentration, meditation and Samadhi at a time, it is called Samyama.

99. Meditation is the key to unlock the door of Moksha.

100. Meditation bestows intuitive knowledge and eternal bliss.

101. Cultivate burning dispassion, burning aspiration or longing for God-realisation. You will have wonderful meditation.

102. Shun Siddhis or psychic powers. They are obstacles in the path of Yoga.

103. Too much sleep, lack of Brahmacharya, laziness, rising up of latent desires, company of worldly people, overwork, overeating are all obstacles in meditation.

104. Meditate on the form of the Lord. This is concrete meditation.

105. Meditate on His attributes. This is abstract meditation.

Pada 20
Samadhi

106. Samadhi is superconscious state.

107. Samadhi is union with God.

108. The state of Samadhi is all bliss.

109. The meditator loses his individuality and becomes identical with the Supreme Self.

110. The state of Samadhi is ineffable.

111. In Savikalpa Samadhi or Samprajnata Samadhi, there is Triputi or the triad, the knower, knowledge and the known.

112. In Savikalpa Samadhi the Samskaras or impressions are not burnt.

113. In Nirvikalpa Samadhi all the impressions are totally burnt.

114. In Asamprajnata Samadhi there is complete inhibition of the functions of the mind.

115. The Yogi attains Kaivalya or Absolute Independence, freedom and perfection, now.

Adhyaya Four

VEDANTA SUTRAS

Pada 1

Nature of Brahman

1. Para Brahman is the only Reality.

2. It is Satchidananda – Existence, Knowledge, Bliss Absolute.

3. It is pure, eternal, infinite, all-pervading consciousness.

4. It is changeless, desireless, secondless, boundless, actionless, taintless, timeless, spaceless, beginningless, endless.

5. Names and forms are not in Brahman.

6. This Brahman was never born, nor will It ever die.

7. It transcends mind, speech and the three Gunas, the three bodies, the three states and the five sheaths.

Pada 2

Bondage and Freedom

8. I am body. I act. I enjoy. She is my wife. He is my son. This is bondage.

9. I am all-pervading Immortal Soul. I am non-actor, non-enjoyer. This is freedom.

10. This is mine. This is bondage. This is not mine. This is freedom. Mine-ness is bondage. Non-mineness is freedom.

11. If the mind is attached to objects of the world, this is bondage. If it is unattached it is liberation.

12. Where there are likes and dislikes there is bondage; where there is neither like nor dislike, there is liberation.

13. Where there is the little self-arrogating 'I' there is bondage; where there is no 'I' there is liberation.

14. Man is bound by 'mine' but he is released by 'not-mine'.

15. The identification of Atman with body and objects constitutes bondage. Identification of one's self with Atman constitutes liberation.

16. The longing after the sensual enjoyment is itself bondage. The renunciation of the same is Moksha.

17. Through Vasanas bondage is caused. With the extinction of all Vasanas knowledge of Brahman will dawn.

18. The identification with the body is the cause of bondage. Freedom from it is liberation.

19. The Jiva appears to be bound and liberated through the force of Avidya or ignorance.

20. When Avidya is destroyed through Brahma Jnana the individual soul merges in the Supreme Soul.

21. There will be no bondage if you do not long for the fruits of actions.

Pada 3

Avidya

22. Ignorance is the cause for pain and sorrow.

23. Annihilate ignorance through Brahma Jnana. All miseries will come to an end.

24. Avidya is ignorance. Avidya is the cause for bondage.

25. Vidya is the cause for liberation.

26. Avidya is the causal body (Karana Sarira) of Jiva.

27. Avidya is impure Sattva (Malina Sattva).

28. It is mixed with Rajas and Tamas.

29. Mind, senses and body are the effects of Avidya.

30. From Avidya is born non-discrimination, from non-discrimination egoism, from egoism likes and dislikes, from likes and dislikes Karma, from Karma body, from body pain.

31. Destroy Avidya, the whole chain will be at once destroyed.

32. Avidya is beginningless but has an end.

33. Avidya ends when Brahma Jnana or knowledge of the self dawns.

34. The 'why' of Avidya is a transcendental mystery. The finite intellect cannot find out the origin of ignorance.

Pada 4

Maya

35. Maya is the inscrutable, illusory power of Brahman.

36. Maya can be crossed through the Grace of God.

37. Maya hides the real, projects the world and makes the unreal appear as real.

38. Slay this Maya through meditation on Atman and Knowledge of Atman.

39. Maya is Suddha Sattva. It has preponderance of Sattva and a trace of Rajas and Tamas.

40. Maya is the causal body (Karana Sarira) of Isvara or the Lord.

41. Maya has two powers, viz., Avarana or the veiling power, and Vikshepa or the projecting power.

42. Maya is of the nature of mind. If one attains Self-realisation, all ideas of the universe, will vanish.

Pada 5

World

43. Just as snake is superimposed on the rope, this world and the body are superimposed on Brahman.

44. Bring a light, the snake vanishes, rope alone remains. Attain knowledge of Self, this world and the body will vanish. Brahman alone remains.

45. The world is an appearance.

46. The world is a Vivarta of Brahman.

47. Time and space are mental modes.

48. Wherever there is mind, there is world.

49. If there is no mind, there is no world.

50. This universe is nothing but the creation of the Sankalpa of the mind.

Pada 6

Jiva

51. The individual soul in essence identical with the Supreme soul.

52. Jiva is individual soul with body, senses, mind, egoism.

53. Jiva is illusory. It is a mere name.

54. Avidya and its effects, viz., body and mind have limited Jiva.

55. Through dawn of Brahma Jnana, the Jiva becomes one with Brahman.

56. Jiva is entangled by the five Kleshas.

57. When the veil of ignorance is removed, the Jiva is freed from individuality and realises the essential Satchidananda nature.

Pada 7

The Three Gunas

58. Sattva is light, harmony, peace, bliss and goodness.

59. Rajas is passion, motion, activity.

60. Tamas is inertia, darkness, carelessness.

61. Sattva is white, Rajas is red and Tamas is black.

62. Each Guna cannot exist by itself.

63. When Sattva manifests, Rajas and Tamas become controlled.

64. When Rajas manifests, Sattva and Tamas become subdued.

65. When Tamas manifests, Sattva and Rajas become subdued.

66. Convert Tamas into Rajas and then convert Rajas into Sattva and transcend Sattva also.

67. Atman is beyond the three Gunas. He is Gunatita.

68. Transcend the three Gunas and become one with Atman. This is Self-realisation.

Pada 8

The Five Sheaths

69. The five sheaths are illusory coverings of the Self.

70. They are: Annamaya Kosa (body), Pranamaya Kosa (vital sheath), Manomaya Kosa (mind), Vijnanamaya Kosa (intellect), and Anandamaya Kosa (causal sheath).

71. Out of ignorance (Avidya) man identifies himself with the sheaths.

72. The unborn, undying, unchanging and conscious Self is not this perishable body inert and subject to birth and death.

73. Even so, the inert Prana, with a beginning and an

end, and which is subject to hunger and thirst, cannot be the all-full, Eternal Consciousness, the Atman.

74. The Ever-Blissful, Eternal Sakshi, always wakeful Atman cannot be the mind which is a restless ocean of passing waves of sorrow, grief, joy, pain and pleasure, and which stops functioning during deep sleep and is powerfully disturbed by a shock.

75. The Infinite Satchidananda Atman cannot be the intellect which is finite; inert and a product of Sattvaguna mixed with Rajas. Intellect shines in the light borrowed from the Self.

76. The Anandamaya Kosa is the seat of ignorance and this, too, though beginningless, has an end at the dawn of Knowledge. Therefore, the Anandamaya Kosa too, is not the Self.

77. The Self, different from the five sheaths, is beginningless, endless, timeless, partless, ever pure, eternal infinite, all-pervading, Satchidananda.

Pada 9

The Three Avasthas

78. The three Avasthas or states are the waking state (Jagrat), dreaming state (Svapna) and the deep sleep state (Sushupti).

79. The state wherein you have the knowledge of the sense objects such as sound, touch, form, taste and smell is called the waking state.

80. The Jiva of the Jagrat state has his seat in the eyes. Vaikhari is his speech. He experiences gross enjoyments. He has Kriya-Sakti and Rajoguna. He is called Visva.

81. You are not the Jagrat state. It belongs to the gross body. You are entirely different from the Jagrat state.

82. The impressions of what you experience in the waking state are revived in the dreaming state.

83. The mind itself creates the dream objects.

84. The seat of Jiva in the dreaming state is throat. He has Madhyama as speech.

85. He has subtle enjoyments and Jnana Sakti.

86. He is called Taijasa.

87. You are entirely distinct from the dreaming state.

88. Mind and the senses are absorbed in the cause-ignorance. This is deep sleep state.

89. The seat of the Jiva in deep sleep is the heart. His speech is Pasyanti. The Guna is Tamas.

90. He is known as Prajna.

91. The deep sleep state does not belong to you. It belongs to the causal body. You are entirely distinct from it.

92. Turiya is the fourth state. This is the state in which the individual soul rests in his own Satchidananda Svaroopa.

Pada 10

Mind

93. Mind is Atma Sakti.

94. The true nature of the mind consists in the Vasanas.

95. The idea of 'I' is the seed of the tree of mind.

96. The sprout which at first germinates from the seed of Ahamkara is termed Buddhi or intellect.

97. Fluctuation of Prana and Vasanas are the two seeds of mind.

98. If the Prana is controlled the mind is also controlled.

99. The mind subjectively is consciousness, while objectively it is the universe.

100. The function of the mind is Sankalpa-Vikalpa.

101. If the thoughts are annihilated, the mind perishes (Manonasa).

102. Enquiry of 'who am I?' will lead to the annihilation of the mind.

Pada 11

OM

103. Om or Pranava is the symbol of Brahman.

104. The whole world has come out of Om. All sounds and languages have come out of Om.

105. Om consists of A U M, Ardhamatra, Nada, Bindu, Kala, Sakti.

106. Om is your real name.

107. A represents waking state, U represents dreaming state, M represents deep sleep state and the Ardhamatra represents the state of Turiya or superconsciousness.

108. Repetition of OM with meaning and Bhava will remove all obstacles on the spiritual path.

109. The Hrasva (short) Pranava destroys all sins.

110. The Deergha (long) Pranava gives Mukti.

111. The Pluta (prolonged) Pranava gives all Siddhis.

112. Meditate on the Om; merge in the Om and become Satchidananda-Svarupa.

Pada 12

Sadhana

113. Equip with the four means of salvation — Viveka, Vairagya, Shad Sampat and Mumukshutva.

114. Then practise Sravana, Manana, and Nididhyasana. You will attain Self-realisation, Atma-Sakshatkara.

115. Approach a Brahma Srotri and Brahma Nishta Guru.

116. Truth or Brahman can be realised or intuited but not understood.

117. Self-realisation is attained through self-discipline, renunciation and meditation.

118. Equip yourself with four means of salvation.

119. When you look at any form take out the essence, reject the name and form.

120. When you work do mentally Japa of Om or Soham. Keep the Atma Bhava, keep the Sakshi Bhava, identifying with Atman.

121. Be self-restrained. Practise Brahmacharya.

122. Enquire 'who am I?' negating the sheaths. Practise Neti, Neti. Separate yourself from the sheaths.

123. Assert I am all-pervading, Immortal, Infinite Atman.

124. Chant Om. Sing Om. Do Japa of Om. Roar Om. Meditate on Om, with Atma Bhava.

125. Practise the Vedantic Yuktis: Anvaya Vyatireka, Adhyaropa Apavada, Bhaga Tyaga Lakshana, Omkara Laya Chintana, Antahkarana Laya Chintana, Pancha Bhuta Laya Chintana.

126. Meditate on the four Maha Vakyas: Prajnanam Brahma, Aham Brahma Asmi, Tat Tvam Asi, Ayam Atma Brahma.

127. Study Upanishads, Brahma Sutras, Panchadasi, Vedanta in Daily Life, Practice of Vedanta, Lectures on Vedanta, Ten Upanishads, Philosophy and meditation on Om, Viveka Chudamani, Gaudapada's Karika.

Pada 13
Samadhi
128. Samadhi is awareness of Reality.

129. Samadhi is superconsciousness. It transcends duality of all kinds.

130. In Samadhi the triad, Known, knowledge and knowable disappear.

131. In Samadhi there is neither 'I' nor 'you', neither 'he' nor 'she', neither 'here' nor 'there', neither 'this' nor 'that', neither 'above' nor 'below'

132. It is a state of fullness and eternal bliss, everlasting joy and perennial peace.

133. In Samadhi there is no consciousness of anything internal or external.

Pada 14

Characteristics of Sage

134. A sage is desireless, fearless and angerless, 'I'-less mine-less.

135. He has equal vision and balanced mind.

136. He has knowledge of past, present and future.

137. He radiates joy and peace.

138. He is possessionless.

139. He is endowed with forgiveness, humility, tolerance, cosmic love, non-covetouness, courage, truthfulness.

Pada 15

Moksha

140. Moksha is freedom from birth and death.

141. Moksha is freedom from the bondage of Karma.

142. Moksha is freedom from the trammels of matter and the thraldom of mind.

143. He who has the four means of salvation can attain Moksha.

144. When the three knots of the heart, Avidya, Kama and Karma are rent asunder, one attains Moksha.

145. Extinction of Sankalpa alone is Moksha.

146. Extinction of Vasanas alone is Moksha.

147. Moksha is not a thing to be achieved. It is already there. You will have to realise this by removing obstructions.

Pada 16

Satchidananda

148. Everyone wants to live for ever; no one wants to die, — because the essential nature of every being is Sat or Existence.

149. From the child who asks the mother: What is this? What is that? to the old man, everyone feels eager to know, to learn — because Infinite Consciousness is his essential nature.

150. Everyone seeks after happiness; no one wants misery, — because everyone's essential nature is Eternal Bliss.

151. Hey Saumya! This Self is of the essential nature of Sat-Chit-Ananda. That thou art. Realise this and be free.

Adhyaya Five

MANOVIJNANA SUTRAS

Pada 1

THE STRUCTURE OF THE MIND
What Is Mind?

1. Now then an exposition of the mind, its nature and control.

2. Mind is Atma-Shakti. Mind is Maya. Mind is born of Prakriti. It is through mind that Brahman or the Absolute manifests Himself as the universe with heterogeneous objects.

3. Mind is inert. It cannot by itself illumine the objects. It borrows its light from Atman or the Self.

4. The body with its organs is no other than the mind.

Mind As the Universe

5. All the visible objects do not really exist. The mind alone shines as the cause of all the manifold created objects.

6. This universe is no other than the mind itself. The Self-light of Para Brahma alone is appearing as the mind or this universe.

7. Mind alone is the universe.

Mind As Sankalpa

8. The form of the mind is Sankalpa alone.

9. The expansion of the mind alone is Sankalpa (thought, imagination).

10. Wherever there is Sankalpa (thought) there does the mind exist.

11. Sankalpa, through its power of differentiation generates this universe.

12. The Sankalpas and Vasanas which you generate enmesh you as in a net.

13. All become subject to bondage through their own Sankalpas and Vasanas like a silk-worm in its cocoon.

14. If the mind turns its back upon discrimination, it entangles itself in the folds of Vasanas, or desires.

Storehouse of Impressions

15. Mind is collection of Samskaras or impressions.

16. The mind goes into modifications according to the latent impressions of the past. These impressions are called Samskaras.

17. Mind is a bundle of Vasanas, Sankalpas and likes and dislikes. If you free yourself from these, the mind dwindles into an airy nothing.

18. Mind is nothing but a bundle of habits, desires and cravings.

19. The mind which is the conditioning vesture of the soul is a storehouse of impressions. It is attached to the pleasures of senses and is tossed about by three Gunas, and hence is liable to disturbances in the form of lust, anger, etc.

20. The true nature of mind is Vasanas or subtle desires.

Size of the Mind

21. Mind is atomic according to the Nyaya school.

22. Mind is all-pervading according to the Raja Yoga School.

23. It is of middling size, same size as that of the body according to the Vedantic school.

Stuff of the Mind

26. Mind is made up of subtle Sattvic matter.

25. It is formed out of the subtlest portion of food.

26. Mind is termed the sixth sense.

Seat of the Mind

27. According to Vedanta, the seat of mind is the heart.

28. According to the Hatha Yoga School, the seat of mind is Ajna Chakra the space between the two eyebrows.

29. Concentration on this Chakra leads to control of mind easily.

30. During waking state the mind occupies the brain.

31. In dream the seat of mind is the throat.

32. In deep sleep the seat of mind is the heart.

The Tree of the Mind

33. The idea of 'I' is the seat of the tree of mind.

34. The sprout which first springs up from this seat of Ahamkara is Buddhi or intellect.

35. From the sprout the ramifying branches called Sankalpas or thoughts have their origin.

36. The poisonous tree of the great Maya's illusion flourishes more and more out of the seed of mind's modifications full of Sankalpas in the soil of variegated enjoyments of the world.

Pada 2

MANY PHASES OF THE MIND

Fourfold Antahkarana

37. When the mind does Sankalpa-Vikalpa, it is called mind.

38. When it discriminates and decides it is called Buddhi or intellect.

39. When it self-arrogates it is Ahamkara, egoism.

40. When it remembers and recollects, it is Chitta.

Strata of Mind

41. Conscious mind is the objective mind. It thinks of objects.

42. Subconscious mind is Chitta. It is the storehouse of impressions.

43. Superconscious mind is the cosmic mind.

The Three Avasthas

44. In the waking state (Jagrat) the mind experiences the external objects.

45. In dream mind itself creates the dream-creatures out of the materials supplied by waking experiences.

46. In deep sleep the mind rests in the causal body or Avidya.

47. In Turiya Avastha the mind is absorbed in Brahman or the Absolute. There is Nirvikalpa Samadhi or superconscious state.

The Three Forms of Mind

48. The Sattvic mind is calm, and harmonious. It intuits, meditates, renounces, enquires and moves towards the Atman.

49. The Rajasic mind is passionate. It wants power, possessions and dominion. It wants to rule over others.

50. The Tamasic mind is heedless. It sleeps. It is full of inertia and darkness.

51. When the Yogi attains Samadhi he rises from the stream of the Gunas and the limitations of the body and mind.

The Sattvic Guna

52. When Sattva is increased a peculiar feeling of

coolness, calmness, contentment and luminosity are experienced by the aspirant.

53. When Sattvic Guna works in the mental sheath, there is wonderful calmness. The tossing of the mind stops and concentration develops.

54. When the Sattva Guna powerfully vibrates in the Vijnanamaya sheath or intellect, there is wonderful knowledge, wonderful memory, wonderful understanding of complex problems.

55. The three Gunas constitute your individuality. They cover your mental, moral, intellectual and spiritual life.

Pada 3

THE DYNAMICS OF THE MIND

Mind: Pure and Impure

56. Suddha Manas or pure mind: this leads to liberation.

57. Asuddha Manas or impure mind: this is the cause for bondage.

58. Suddha Manas is filled with Sattva or purity and divine virtues.

59. Asuddha Manas is filled with impurities such as lust, greed, jealousy, hatred, etc.

Functions of the Mind

60. It is the actions of the mind that are truly termed Karmas.

61. The function of the mind is Sankalpa-Vikalpa, thinking and doubting.

62. It is the mind that really sees, hears, smells, tastes and feels.

63. Mind can do the five functions of the five senses of perception or Knowledge.

64. Mind connects itself with the five senses of perception and enjoys all sense-objects.

Power of the Mind

65. The mind has the potency of creating or undoing the world in the twinkling of an eye.

66. Mind creates the world according to its own Sankalpa or thought.

67. It is the mind that creates this universe; *manomatram jagat; manah kalpitam jagat.*

68. Through the play of the mind, a Kalpa is reckoned by it as a moment and vice versa.

69. Like a dream generating another dream in it the mind having no visible form generates existent visibles.

Play of the Mind

70. The mind assumes the form of any object it intensely thinks of.

71. Through the play of the mind in objects, nearness appears to be a great distance and vice versa.

72. In introspection a portion of the mind studies another portion of the mind.

73. The senses can do nothing without the cooperation of the mind.

74. It is the mind that causes bondage and release. Devoted to sense-objects it causes bondage, devoted to the Lord it creates freedom and release.

75. With the growth of the mind, the pains increase, with its extinction, there will be infinite bliss.

76. Mind can do or attend to only one thing at a time.

The Mischievous Mind

77. Mind is the slayer of Atman or the supreme Self.

78. Mind is the birth-place of desire.

79. Mind ever whirls far and wide in vain in sensual objects like a strolling street dog.

80. This puerile mind which ever rises and falls with the ebb and flow of desires, fancies this illusory universe to be true through its ignorance.

81. Ever thirsting after fresh Vishayas or sense-objects the mind is more restless than monkeys.

The Tainted Mind

82. The stainful mind has not the benevolence to consider other's happiness as its own. So it is ever reeling.

83. This mind has not the complacency to rejoice at another's virtues. Therefore there is no internal contentment.

84. The mind becomes unstable and restless through desires for objects.

85. When the mind is not centred in the Atman, man desires for objects.

86. A mind attached to the pleasures of the senses leads to misery in the shape of births and deaths.

Ripples of the Mind

87. Vritti is a wave in the mind-lake.

88. Lust, anger, etc., are evil Vrittis in the mind.

89. Faith, devotion, dispassion, discrimination, courage, mercy are good Vrittis in the mind.

90. Jealousy is a form of continuous anger.

91. Arrogance is a form of pride.

92. Insolence is overbearing nature.

93. Irshya is a form of jealousy.

94. Greed intensifies desire, destroys peace of mind and retards spiritual progress.

95. Vismriti is the confused understanding of one who is swayed by evil propensities like passion, anger, greed, etc.

96. Cultivate good Vrittis. The evil Vrittis will die by themselves. Do not attack the evil Vrittis directly.

Pada 4
METHODS OF MIND-CONTROL
Removal of Three Mental Defects

97. The three defects or Doshas of the mind are Mala (impurities such as lust, anger, greed), Vikshepa (tossing or oscillation) and Avarana (veil of ignorance).

98. Mala is removed by selfless service.

99. Vikshepa is removed by Upasana, Trataka and Pranayama.

100. Avarana or veil is removed by study and practice of Vedanta.

The Difficulty of Mind-control

101. It is possible to drink the contents of the ocean, walk over fire and water, fly in the air, eradicate the Himalayas to its root, and swallow the flaming fire, but it is difficult to control the mind.

102. The struggle with the mind is most distasteful and bitter in the first stage of the Sadhana.

103. Mind cannot be controlled by mere human effort. The grace of the Lord and Guru is necessary.

104. Control of the mind is the first step to spirituality. Victory over the mind means victory over the world.

105. Self-conquest or conquest of the mind is the greatest victory.

106. Yoga aims at arriving at the silence of the mind which makes possible the right meditation.

Conquest by Yoga and Jnana

107. You can control the mind through Yoga and Jnana. For some, it is easy to control the mind through Yoga and Jnana. For some it is easy to control the mind through Yoga, for some through Jnana.

108. All the practices which go in the name of Yoga are just to concentrate the mind and still it.

109. When the mind goes outward, restrain and steady it on the innermost Self or Atman that dwells in the chambers of your heart.

110. When your mind is agitated withdraw into silence and regain the inner calm and tranquillity.

111. The mind attains through discrimination, enquiry and meditation, the peace of the Eternal.

112. Dispassion, discrimination, renunciation and meditation are all deadly enemies of the mind.

113. Have a balanced mind. Again and again practise the state. Rest in Atman. May you be immovable as a rock.

114. Enquire who am I? Do Brahmavichara. Enquire into the nature of the Absolute. Meditate ceaselessly on the all-pervading immortal Atman. The mind will be absorbed into the source.

115. Meditate on OM or the Mahavakya, "Aham Brahmasmi"; "I am Brahman". This will put to end all mental operations and bring about Self-realisation or Atma-Sakshatkara.

Need for Intelligent Methods

116. Do not try to control the mind through violent methods. You will miserably and hopelessly fail.

117. Conquer the mind slowly and carefully through intelligent means. Overcome desires and aversion by

means of meditation. Enter silence and rest peacefully for ever.

118. The mind must be slowly and carefully conquered by the power of the will diverted from the path of unrighteousness to the path of meditation.

119. The impurities of the mind are removed and Tamas is annihilated by the ceaseless practice of selfless service, feeling all the time that service is the worship of the Lord.

120. Mind is the dividing wall between the individual soul and the Supreme Soul. If the mind is destroyed the individual soul becomes identical with the Supreme Soul.

121. Mind in its natural state is endowed with purity, immortality and peace.

122. When the oil in a lamp becomes exhausted, the flame is absorbed in its cause, similarly, the mind deprived of the support of all objective pleasure seeking centres, becomes calm and gets absorbed in Brahman or the Absolute.

Pratipakshabhavana

123. Do not fight evil. Replace it by the opposite good, and the evil automatically will vanish.

124. Do not try to drive away impure thoughts. The more you try, the more they will return. Entertain pure thoughts.

125. Pure Vasanas tend to develop the true Jnana or wisdom.

126. Annihilate the impure or lower mind with the help of the pure or higher mind and transcend the higher mind also.

127. Fill the mind with divine thoughts. The impure thoughts will gradually vanish by themselves.

128. Like an iron shaping another iron, the mind should correct and mould your impure mind.

Conquest by Abhyasa

129. Steadying or fixing the mind on one point is called Abhyasa.

130. If you eradicate all desires and thoughts the mind will die by itself.

131. Dispassion and inner and outer control must be practised together with intense meditation on Atman.

132. When the mind wanders bring it back and try to fix it on the Divine Light within the centre of your heart.

133. Detach the mind from all thoughts of sense-objects through Vairagya (dispassion) and centre it upon the Lord.

134. Vairagya (dispassion) and Abhyasa (concentration and meditation) are the weapons to annihilate this turbulent mind.

The Role of Pranayama

135. The mind attains steadiness through the practice of Pranayama or regulation of breath.

136. Slay this mind through the destruction of the Vasanas or the control of Prana and Brahmavichara, (enquiry into the nature of Brahman).

137. The mind is purified by the practice of selfless service, Japa, Tapas, right conduct, practice of Yama, Niayama and meditation.

138. Overcome sleep by regulating your diet and taking only light, Sattvic food and by the practice of Asanas and Pranayama.

139. As gold melted in fire is purified of its dross, so can the mind be purified by control of Prana or the vital airs.

Pada 5

MASTERY OF THE MIND

Disentanglement of the Mind

140. He who masters the mind will attain liberation or freedom from births and deaths.

141. With the destruction of mind, all the three periods of time vanish into nothing.

142. If the mind is purged of all its impurities, then it will become very calm and all delusions attendant with its birth and death will be destroyed.

143. True emancipation results from the disenthralment of the mind.

Peace of Mind

144. When the mind becomes inaccessible to evil thoughts and keeps away from the lure of sense-objects, it grasps the eternal Truth and becomes the abode of everlasting peace.

145. The mind which is not agitated by lust is always tranquil.

146. Real peace can be found only in the control of desire, in the turning of the mind to the one enduring Reality, God.

The Barrier of Egoism

147. Ahamkara is the source of all dangers, pains and sorrows in this world. It is evanescent. It has its seat in the mind. It is idiotic in its nature. It is without discrimination and intelligence.

148. Egoism is a formidable chronic disease. It can be destroyed by the potent injection of self-surrender to God.

149. From inadvertence (Pramada) comes delusion,

from delusion egoism, from egoism bondage, and all the consequent sorrow that one is heir to.

150. The notions 'I'-ness and 'mine'-ness have no real existence.

151. 'Mine'-ness is death. Freedom from 'mine'-ness is immortality or Life Eternal.

152. Heedlessness is dangerous because it is the cause of egoism, bondage and sorrow.

153. If the modifications of the mind which lean on sensual pleasure be destroyed, then Atman divested of Ahamkara (egoism) becomes the All-pervading Reality or Brahman.

154. Ahamkara causes the Self to think of itself as 'I' and of objects as 'mine'. It is the principle of individuation.

The Deluded Mind

155. Even the worst thing appears to be very pleasant when the mind is deluded.

156. As the mind does not consider other's pains as its own there arises no compassion in it.

157. Whatever is thought of by one at the time of death, that will be realised by him afterwards.

158. Every thought, every feeling which does not vibrate love, clouds the understanding and takes you away from God.

159. The expansion of the mind's thoughts towards objects is bondage; while the abandoning of the Sankalpas is emancipation.

The True Source of Delight

160. There is no bliss in the object. When the desire is fulfilled the mind becomes still momentarily and is turned inward. The Atman reflects in its true form as bliss in the mind thus turned.

161. When you attain a desired object, the mind is stilled for a moment and the reflection of bliss from Atman becomes manifest.

162. When the restless waves of the mind subside, then arises gradually divine bliss.

163. If the modifications of the mind which lean towards sensual pleasures are destroyed, then the individual soul attains supreme Peace.

164. If the mind which flies from one object to another is slain with the sword of discrimination, then the Self-shining Para-Brahman or the Absolute will be realised.

165. The more the mind is withdrawn from the outer world the more it is making headway in the realm of Atman or eternal bliss.

166. He who has freed himself from the fluctuations of his mind comes into possession of the supreme Nishta (meditation) and bliss Immortal.

Liberation by Mind-dissolution

167. With the annihilation of this Sankalpa, all conceptions of the differences between the Seer and the Seen will vanish. Then Para-Brahman or the Reality will shine by itself in its pristine glory and splendour.

168. A contented mind is ever calm and serene.

169. A mind which though enjoying the diverse objects, does not enjoy them is Brahman Itself.

170. If the mind is destroyed the individual soul becomes identical with the Supreme Soul.

171. When the mind is purified and concentrated, meditation on the form of the Lord should be earnestly taken to.

172. When the mind is completely dissolved, liberation follows automatically.

Pada 6

THE PROCESS OF MEDITATION

Method of Meditation

173. Meditation is a process by which there arises intuitive experience or spiritual Aparoksha (direct) Anubhava or experience.

174. Practise silent meditation. Attain spiritual development and Self-realisation.

175. Sit erect in a position of ease. Repeat OM, meditating on its meaning. Free the mind from all distracting thoughts and desires.

176. If your meditation is imperfect, examine your heart. They may be still undercurrent of Vasanas or desires, attachment and egoism. The senses may still be turbulent. Still there may be craving for sense-pleasures.

177. The practice of meditation is the great scientific method of knowledge.

Importance of Meditation

178. There is no knowledge without meditation. The Yogi churns his own soul. Truth becomes manifest.

179. Meditation is the most important aspect of religious life. Right meditation is very important. It is a process of canalising the mind to take the form of the object of meditation.

180. Meditation on Brahman bestows immortality. There is no other way to Immortality.

Goal of Meditation

181. The object of meditation is the realisation of the transcendental consciousness through intuition.

182. He who follows the path of meditation knows his Self as Divine and one with God.

183. Meditation brings you nearer to Truth than anything else.

184. Meditation is Dhyana. It leads to the summit of Samadhi or superconscious state.

185. When the transcendence of the Gunas has taken place through the evolution of intuition, the meditation ceases.

186. After reaching the Goal, the Yogi does not meditate. There is no object to meditate upon, because everywhere he sees the all-pervasive Lord.

Benefits of Meditation

187. Even a little meditation saves you from fear of death.

188. Constant practice of meditation will bring tranquillity and peace within.

189. Meditation fills the mind with cheerful, powerful, Sattvic thoughts.

190. By sustained meditation on the form of the Lord, the devotee will acquire the deepest love for the Lord.

191. In meditation you get directly an abundant supply of Sattva from the Lord.

192. An aspirant who meditates regularly enjoys peace, tranquillity, joy and a feeling of independence.

193. Meditation is a great tonic and revitaliser. Have serene meditation in the calm hours of early dawn and quiet hours of evening twilight.

194. By practice of meditation all the lower desires vanish all personal thoughts will cease. There is only desire to be one with the Lord.

Obstacles in Meditation

195. Thinking of the past and anxiety about the future is a hindrance in meditation.

196. Memory or recollection is a great obstacle in meditation.

197. Meditation must be deep, regular, more serious and continuous.

198. Ignore psychic experiences and keep the mind alert and fixed on the object of meditation.

199. Through Vairagya and meditation the senses are weakened and the mind merges itself in the Supreme.

200. Be moderate in food. Dwell in solitude. Meditate, leave anger; abandon pride.

201. Yama, Niayama, Asana, Pranayama become preliminary to meditation.

Mind in Meditation

202. In meditation the mind is turned back upon itself. The mind stops all the thought-waves.

203. The moment the mind is restrained for the purpose of meditation, the impressions, the sensations of the past constantly disturb the meditation.

204. When the spiritual vision is developed through Sattva and meditation you will be able to see the subtler existence, the Devatas and the soul.

205. When you develop intuition through meditation, realisation of Atman takes place.

Self-realisation by Meditation

206. Meditate on the innermost Self ceaselessly. The mind will be absorbed in Brahman. You will attain Self-realisation.

207. Slay the ego or the false self. Sit motionless and calm. Meditate and realise Atman.

208. When you have considerable progress in meditation, you lost the awareness of the process mediation. You even cease to be aware of yourself, what remains is only the object of meditation. There is only awareness of pure consciousness.

209. Intuition merges the subject and object of knowledge together with the process of knowing into the Supreme Brahman.

210. Learn to find eternal peace and everlasting bliss in meditation on the Atman or the Self Supreme.

211. He who practises meditation regularly and vigorously enters into Samadhi and attains a direct cognition of the all-full Jnana or Wisdom. He attains the supreme state of Jivanmukta devoid of this illusory universe though existent for others.

212. Meditate in silence regularly. You will get inspiration, peace and spiritual strength. You will catch the glory of God and the splendour of Truth. You will feel the immanence of Truth.

Pada 7

TWO FORMS OF SAMADHI

Meaning of Samadhi

213. Samadhi is a state of full wisdom. It is union with the Absolute.

214. In the Samadhi or the state where there are no limitations, there is nothing like the knower and the known. It is all a homogeneous experience.

215. In the state of Samadhi the mind merges with the Absolute or Brahman. Individuality melts. Everlasting Bliss is attained. The sage is free from pain, sorrow, fear and delusion.

216. Samadhi is all unity or Atman alone.

217. The state where there is absolute consciousness, where the mind does not seek or is at perfect rest, where the knower and the known have become one is Samadhi.

218. Through the annihilation of the modifications of the mind, you can attain Samadhi.

Savikalpa Samadhi

219. In Savikalpa Samadhi there is the consciousness, "I am meditating;" "Brahman is the object of meditation."

220. In Savikalpa Samadhi, there is the consciousness of the knower, knowledge and the known.

221. In the case of Savikalpa Samadhi there is the consciousness of duality but it is superficial and only apparent.

222. Savikalpa Samadhi is a stage of preparation. Nirvikalpa Samadhi is the goal.

Nirvikalpa Samadhi

224. When the mind ceases functioning, when all thoughts subside, when all consciousness of the body and the outer world is effaced from the mind, the individual soul merges in the supreme soul. This is the Nirvikalpa Samadhi.

225. Abandon all Sankalpas and become a Nirvikalpa.

226. A man who is dreaming in his sleep experiences many sufferings, but when he wakes, feels no concern with any of them. Even so, he who rests in Nirvikalpa Samadhi or Atman will be beyond all the effects of Prakriti.

227. In Nirvikalpa Samadhi no individual consciousness remains, as the individual consciousness is merged in the universal consciousness.

228. In Nirvikalpa Samadhi there is the absolute absence of the triad of knower, knowledge and the known.

Pada 8

GOSPEL OF GOD-REALISATION
The State of Spiritual Freedom

229. Salvation is not in heaven or any other plane. It lies in a purified mind.

230. Freedom from the thraldom of mind, desires likes and dislikes, is emancipation.

231. Moksha comes where there is no desire for Moksha.

232. Moksha is not mere negative freedom from pain, misery, from the cycle of births and deaths but is the positive state of infinite, eternal, supreme bliss.

Conditions for Moksha

233. The qualification for Moksha is not mere learning, but the sterling qualities of discrimination and dispassion.

234. Only when the mind is serene you can attain Self-realisation.

235. Balance of mind or mental equipoise is an indispensable element in spiritual life. Develop this again and again.

236. A disciplined and one-pointed mind is essential for God-realisation.

Need for Complete Purity

237. If the pure Vasanas cling to you, you will easily attain Self-realisation or the immaculate Brahmic seat through them, but if you have impure Vasanas, pains will be generated.

238. A mind which is free from craving for sensual pleasure makes the final beatitude.

239. Devotion, discrimination, dispassion,

self-surrender, sinlessness and meditation lead to the goal of Mukti or emancipation.

240. As a small bulb cannot withstand excessive electrical voltage so the aspirant's nerves are not ready to receive the cosmic current when his mind is not thoroughly purified.

241. If he receives the infinite divine light when his vessel is not ready he will feel burning as if every cell were on fire. The vessel may burst as it cannot hold the great light.

242. Cultivate purity of character, self-confidence, hospitality, affection and sweet speech. Meditate regularly. You will soon attain God-realisation.

Spiritual Experience

243. Spiritual experience is proportionate to spiritual fitness.

244. Spiritual progress is not measured by your psychic powers, but only by the depth of your bliss in meditation.

245. Have a mind purified by the instruction of your preceptor and the practice of spiritual discipline. You will soon attain Self-realisation.

Mind and Self-realisation

246. Self-realisation can be effected through the mind alone after abandoning its Samskaras and Vikalpas.

247. Self-realisation is the only means to freedom. It cuts the knot of egoism in the heart.

248. Renounce Moha (attachment). Moha is rooted in desire. He who renounces attachment attains God-realisation.

249. Eternal bliss arises when the mind merges in Brahman or the Absolute.

250. If the mind be divested of the thoughts of "I", then

through meditation on Atman you can attain immortality and bliss eternal.

251. When the mind becomes pure through spiritual discipline you will realise Brahman as a homogenous, pure, non-dual Consciousness.

Adhyaya Six

NEETI SUTRAS

Pada 1

FOUNDATIONS OF MORAL LIFE

Introductory: Morality and Spirituality

1. Ethics is an enquiry into the nature of good and is concerned with an analysis of the concepts of good and bad, virtue and vice, right and wrong.

2. Moral law is the expression of the perfection of God. It is the voice of God in man.

3. Morality is the basis for the realisation of Atman or Supreme Self.

4. Self-realisation is the ultimate meaning of ethics.

5. Ethics is right living.

6. Right and wrong are to be determined not by the objective consequences but by the nature of subjective intention of the doer.

7. God looks to the motive of the doer.

8. Science has to be supplemented by ethics, religion, Yoga and Vedanta.

9. Religious and moral instructions must be imparted in schools and colleges.

10. A life of pure thought and virtuous deeds will bring you nearer to God quickly.

11. The practice of truth and self-control leads to Moksha or the final emancipation.

12. Where there are kindness, humility and purity, there

spirituality springs up, saintliness shines, divinity descends and perfection manifests itself.

Importance of Moral Character

13. Character is the essence of man.

14. Out of righteousness springs wealth; out of righteousness springs happiness.

15. Truth and justice alone triumph in the end; injustice and falsehood perish.

16. Kill Dharma and you will kill yourself. Save Dharma and you save yourself.

17. Virtue is the key to blessedness. Vice is the gateway to hell and misery.

18. No Yoga, Samadhi or Kaivalya is possible without ethical perfection.

19. That which is ethically good helps man to attain freedom, perfection and everlasting bliss.

20. That which is ethically bad brings misery, suffering and lower birth to man.

21. Thought determines character. Character is life's pillar.

22. Man needs now no more degrees, but character, no more study but wisdom.

23. He who has blameless character and good behaviour can realise the Truth quickly.

24. Chitta-suddhi or purification of the mind is an indispensable condition for attaining success in Yoga and Samadhi.

Essentials of Moral Life

25. Think truly. Speak truly. Live truly. Act truly.

26. Adaptability, kind speech, pure conduct, patience — these are the four fundamental virtues.

27. You may possess all the virtues but if you do not have humility, all that counts for nothing.

28. Good nature, benevolence, truthfulness and justice are the foundation of character.

29. Courage, forgiveness, control of mind, avoidance of misappropriation, purity of mind and body, sense-control, intelligence, learning, truthfulness and absence of anger are the characteristics of virtue and good conduct. Practise them constantly and assiduously.

30. Mercy, truthfulness, cosmic love, purity, self-control, courage, tolerance, honesty, generosity, yearning for God-realisation, serenity, and discrimination are the ingredients of good character.

31. Do as you would be done by. This is the gist of ethics.

32. Be good. Do good. This is right conduct. This is the essence of ethics and morality.

The Universal Maxims

33. Do good to him who hates you. Return good for evil.

34. Do not return a blow by a blow, nor a curse by a curse. Shower blessings in return for blows and curses.

35. Never do anything of which you will have occasion to repent.

36. The act which does not do good to others, or that act which one has to feel shame, should never be done.

37. Shun these seven: anger, immorality, ignorance, conceit, aimlessness, covetousness and sloth.

38. Develop these seven: faith, energy, strength of will, courage, patience, selflessness and insight.

39. Purify, concentrate, meditate and realise now and here. This is your foremost duty. All other duties are secondary.

40. Non-injury, truthfulness, non-covetousness, purity and control of the senses are the common duties of all men.

Pada 2

THE STRUCTURE OF DHARMA

The Meaning of Dharma

41. That which elevates you and takes you nearer to God is right action or Dharma.

42. Dharma is righteous living. Dharma supports life.

43. The actions performed in accordance with the injunctions of the Scriptures are right.

44. That which leads you to the goal or Moksha is Dharma.

45. Dharma means that which upholds this world or the people of the world or the whole creation.

46. Dharma means the Achara or the regulation of life.

The Nature of Adharma

47. That which brings you down and takes you away from God is wrong action or Adharma.

48. The actions done against the injunctions of Scriptures are wrong.

49. Adharma will bring the destruction of its adherents and then suffers defeat at the hands of Dharma.

50. Adharma or unrighteousness cannot survive for a long time.

God and Dharma

51. God is the centre of Dharma.

52. Dharma is the Eternal Divine Law of the Supreme Lord.

53. The only authority in the matter of Dharma is the Vedas.

78

54. That which is Dharma is verily the Truth.

55. Realise the Truth by practising righteousness.

The Limbs of Dharma

56. Truth, compassion, Tapas and charity are the four feet of Dharma.

57. The path of Dharma is extremely subtle and difficult of comprehension. Therefore follow the teachings of the scriptures and instructions of sages in a judicious way.

58. Dharma includes all external deeds as well as thoughts and other mental practices which tend to elevate the character of a man.

59. Dharma is the basis of Tapas or austerity.

Practice of Dharma

60. To violate the law of Dharma is sin.

61. Where there is no Dharma, there is no happiness.

62. Nothing can bring about harmony, universal peace and prosperity except Dharma.

63. Founded upon Dharma, politics and nation-building are ensured prosperity, success, glory and growth.

64. Based upon Dharma family-life will be happy, useful and divine.

65. Abandon not Dharma at any cost, even at the risk of life.

The General Dharma

66. Truthfulness, contentment, self-restraint, non-stealing, purity, control of anger, discrimination between the right and wrong, between the real and the unreal, spiritual knowledge and control of the senses come under the general or universal Dharma.

67. The six characteristics of Dharma are the bestowing of gifts to deserving person, fixing one's thoughts on the

Lord, adoration of one's parents, offering a portion of the daily meal to all creatures and giving a morsel of food to cows.

68. Saamaanya Dharma is the general Dharma or the general law for all men.

69. Forgiveness, truthfulness, control of the mind, purity, practice of charity, control of the senses, non-violence, service of Guru, visiting the places of pilgrimage, compassion, simpleness, absence of greed, worship of the gods are the essentials of Saamaanya Dharma for all men.

Pada 3

MORAL INSTRUCTIONS

Avoidance of Tricky Ways

70. Do not take recourse to base tricks and mean craftiness. Be frank and straightforward.

71. Obey the laws and commandments of scriptures implicitly.

72. Selfishness, cheating, double-dealing, diplomacy, hypocrisy and falsehood are the constant companions of greed.

73. Do not take equal seat with your Guru, teachers and elders.

74. Be obedient to your father and mother. They are the visible representatives of God.

Base of Moral Life

75. Abstain from injury in thought, word and deed.

76. The ideal of life is purity, endurance, devotion, self-abnegation, self-restraint, renunciation and Self-realisation.

77. Fasting destroys sins and purifies the heart. It is also a penance.

78. Have steadiness of purpose. Be resolute. Be fiery in your determination. Have an iron-will.

79. As iron rod that is in contact with the fire receives the properties of the fire; so also the individual soul who meditates on the Lord and recites His Name attains the qualities of the Lord.

Forms of Charity

80. To pray for another is charity. To serve another is charity.

81. To be kind and loving is charity. To forget and forgive some harm done to you is charity.

82. A kind word said to a suffering man is charity.

83. Generosity is the sister virtue of charity.

Goodness and Godliness

84. This body is meant for the good of others.

85. Treat a deserving guest hospitably. First give to him and then eat for yourself.

86. Supreme goodness is God. Lead the life of goodness.

87. To live in perfect goodness is to dissolve in the Infinite.

88. Vidya destroys Avidya. Vidya is wisdom of Atman. Avidya is nescience or ignorance.

89. A life of pure thoughts and virtuous deeds will bring you nearer to God quickly.

Principles of Actions

90. Revere your superiors, love your equals, and protect and raise your inferiors.

91. Never break your promise, but be quick to perform it.

92. Have no secrets of your own, but do not expose the secrets of others.

93. Frankly admit your faults and mistakes. You will grow in spirituality.

94. Overcome anger by love, evil by good, greed by liberality, fear by courage, falsehood by truth, pride by humility, infatuation by enquiry, harshness by gentleness and sweetness, immorality by morality, and worldliness by divinity.

Pada 4
SATYAM, AHIMSA, BRAHMACHARYA
Volume of Truthfulness

95. Truthfulness is the first pillar in the temple of Self-realisation.

96. There is no penance like truth.

97. From truth originate righteousness and self-control.

98. Truth is the gateway to the Kingdom of God.

99. Righteousness is the best acquisition of man. It is the world's highest wealth.

The Branches of Righteousness

100. Out of righteousness springs wealth; out of righteousness springs happiness.

101. Ahimsa, Brahmacharya, purity, justice, harmony, forgiveness, peace are forms of truth.

102. Impartiality, self-control, forgiveness, modesty, endurance, kindness, renunciation, meditation, dignity, fortitude, compassion and abstention from injury are the various forms of truth.

103. Righteousness is the support of the entire world.

104. Righteousness forms the bed-rock of all religions.

The Roots of Righteousness

105. Righteousness and propriety arise from the inner springs of the human hearts.

106. Control over passions constitutes the essence of truth.

107. You must be free from greed and lust if you want to tread the path of righteousness.

108. There is truth where righteousness is.

109. Righteousness is the divine path.

110. Wealth, beauty, honour, and youth fade away but the life of righteousness will never decay.

111. Bliss is for him who is righteous.

112. God is righteousness.

Ahimsa As a Spiritual Force

113. Ahimsa is not to be regarded as a mere occasion or as a matter of policy. It must become an all important principle, dominating your life.

114. If you are established in Ahimsa, you have attained all virtues.

115. You cannot practise Ahimsa without practising truth.

116. Ahimsa is a great spiritual force. It is cosmic love.

117. Ahimsa is not mere negative non-injury. It is positive cosmic love.

118. Ahimsa, Satyam and Brahmacharya symbolise the processes of avoiding sin, sticking to virtue and self-purification.

119. Practise Ahimsa (non-violence). If you injure any other creature, you really injure yourself, because the whole world is nothing but your own Self.

The Need for Brahmacharya

120. Brahmacharya is to the Yogi what electricity is to an electric bulb.

121. Without Brahmacharya, the aspirant cannot at all progress or rise up in the path of Yoga.

122. Brahmacharya makes spiritual unfoldment possible.

123. Brahmacharya provides the force or the motive power for the seeker's ascent to the higher planes.

124. Let mercy soften your heart. Let virtue gladden your heart. Let Brahmacharya purify your heart.

125. The basis of body-building and spiritual growth is Brahmacharya.

126. Brahmacharya lies at the very heart of Tapas or Yoga.

Pada 5

SELF-CONTROL, VIRTUE AND LOVE

Constituents of Self-control

127. Forgiveness, patience, abstention from injury, impartiality, truth, sincerity, serenity, control of the senses, cleverness, mildness, modesty, firmness, generosity, liberality, freedom from anger, contentment, sweetness of words, benevolence, freedom from malice — all these combined make up self-control.

128. Self-denial or refraining from the worldly enjoyments forms the essence of self-control.

129. Self-control increases your energy. It is indispensable for leading a true ethical life.

Conquest of Anger

130. Anger is the worst fire. It burns your heart.

Extinguish this fire through enquiry, love, forgiveness and patience.

131. Try to govern your temper. Control your anger. Anger is the enemy of devotion, peace and wisdom.

132. Anger takes its origin from covetousness. It disappears through forgiveness.

133. Anger begets many vices such as injustice, violence, harshness, murder, quarrel, fighting, etc.

134. From covetousness originates anger. From covetousness grows lust.

Rewards of Virtue

135. Virtue conduces to happiness, vice to pain.

136. Virtue is the root of happiness.

137. Goodness is the way to true happiness.

138. Virtue will pave the way for you to march into the kingdom of eternal bliss.

139. A man without virtuous qualities is a dead man while living.

Divinity and Virtue

140. Virtue has divinity behind it.

141. Wherever is divinity, there is virtue.

142. A life of pure thoughts and virtuous deeds will bring you nearer to God very quickly.

143. The path of virtue lies in the renunciation of arrogance, pride and egoism.

Essence of Virtue

144. Wisdom of the Self is the right fruit of the beautiful flower of virtue.

145. Asceticism, forgiveness, mercy, truth, self-control and pure love are different forms of virtue.

146. Sticking to promise is a great vow. It is a great virtue.

147. Justice, temperance, courage and purity are the four great virtues.

148. The very root and the core of all moral discipline is mental purification through refraining from all evil actions and the active practice of virtue.

149. Brahma Jnana is the best acquisition. Contentment is the best happiness. Mercy is the virtue of virtues.

Love: The Greatest Power

150. Only one Soul dwells in all beings. Therefore, love all as your own Self.

151. To love God is to love all. To love all is to love God.

152. True love is the greatest Power on this earth. It rules without a sword and binds without a cord.

153. He who sees everyone in himself and himself in everyone, no more injures the self by the self. He sees sameness in all.

Pada 6
PHASES OF MORAL THOUGHT
Motive in Moral Life

154. The inner motives of a man form the seed and root of all his life's activities.

155. If an action is done with a pure motive, it will purify the heart and lead to the attainment of the final emancipation.

156. Before you perform an action scrutinise your motive. If there is selfishness, give up that action.

157. It is the motive that counts in the performance of an action.

158. An action done with a selfish motive binds to the wheel of births and deaths.

Purity of Nature

159. Purity is freedom from desires.

160. Lust imprisons the soul, but purity liberates and elevates.

161. Purity is the first requisite for God-realisation. Therefore, cultivate purity.

162. In purity is the secret of God-realisation, in self-restraint the strength of character, and in dispassion spiritual progress.

163. If you wish to be strong, be pure.

Morality and Immorality

164. Morality is the gateway to religion.

165. Morality is the gateway to bliss Immortal.

166. The aim of morality is to raise man to the level of Divinity by transforming his brutal nature.

167. It is immoral to drink liquor.

168. It is immoral to hurt others.

169. It is immoral to burst out in anger.

170. It is immoral to tell lies or deceive others.

171. It is immoral to entertain lustful thoughts.

Conduct and Character

172. Conduct is personal behaviour.

173. Character expresses itself as conduct.

174. Conduct reveals the character of the man.

175. Conduct is the outer expression of character.

176. Conduct and character are inseparable from each other.

177. The sum-total of his virtues forms his character.

178. Build your character by cultivation of virtues.

179. Every action affects the character of a man.

Sources of Moral Thought

180. Tread the footsteps of saints, sages and learned men.

181. Walk in the path of duty. Attain knowledge of Atman.

182. All saints think alike, talk alike and act alike. Their level of consciousness is the same.

183. Learn how to live rightly. Learn how to lead the life Divine, by sitting at the Lotus-Feet of a preceptor or Guru.

184. Learn from the saints and sages all rules of conduct and practise them.

185. Learn good morals from the Sacred Scriptures and saints and follow them implicitly with reverence and faith. This will lead you to eternal Peace.

Some Moral Lessons

186. Obstinacy is a dangerous vice. It is not strength of will. It is Tamasic foolishness on account of pig-headedness.

187. Mercy to all creatures, control of anger, charity, freedom from malice, and pride, restraint of senses, and to follow the teachings of Sastras and sages constitute the praiseworthy behaviour.

188. Satsanga, discrimination, dispassion, cultivation of nobility, generosity, charity, integrity, and honesty will eradicate covetousness.

189. There never was, there never will be, a man who always praised or a man who is always censured.

190. A life of sacrifice demands renunciation and selflessness.

191. There is no vice greater than backbiting, no sin

greater than uttering falsehood, no penance greater than Ahimsa, and no death worse than a dishonourable life.

192. Speech is the mirror of the soul. As a man speaks, so is he.

193. Regulation of daily life leads to longevity, prosperity, health and eternal bliss.

194. Courage and patience are the twin qualities of a real aspirant.

Benefits of Moral Character

195. Contentment is the supreme wealth. It cools the fire of greed.

196. Ethics leads to restraint of the lower self and thereby the mind is made calm.

197. Falsehood, cruel acts, immoral life, crookedness, and deceitfulness kill the conscience.

198. Greed clouds understanding and makes man blind.

199. Covetousness begets loss of judgment, deception, pride, haughtiness, malice, vindictiveness, shamelessness, loss of virtues and infamy.

200. The practice of endurance, steadfastness, control of senses, and other Sadachara Karmas (common duties) aim in making a man self-supporting, independent and free from external bondage, physical and social.

201. Virtuous acts, nobility, generosity, charity, benevolence, acts of mercy, practice of truthfulness, Brahmacharya, and Ahimsa sharpen the conscience.

202. Practise pure love, truthfulness and self-restraint. Your mental powers will be increased, and your physical well-being will be improved.

Adhyaya Seven

MANTRA YOGA SUTRAS

Pada 1

THE SCIENCE OF MANTRA YOGA

Definition of Mantra

1. *Mananat trayate iti mantrah.* By the Manana or constant thinking or recollection of a Mantra one is released from the round of births and deaths; so it is called Mantra.

2. A Mantra is so-called because God is achieved by the mental process (meditation, reflection).

3. The root '*man*' in the word Mantra comes from the first syllable of that word, meaning 'to think' and '*tra*' from '*trai*' meaning to 'protect' or 'free' from the bondage of births and deaths.

4. Mantra Yoga is an exact science.

Rishis and Siddha Mantras

5. A Mantra has a Rishi who gave it to the world; a metre which governs the inflection of the voice; and a Devata; the Bija or seed which gives it a special power.

6. Rishis attained God-realisation through recitation of a Mantra.

7. Such a Mantra is a Siddha Mantra.

8. OM Namah Sivaya, OM Namo Narayanaya, OM Namo Bhagavate Vaasudevaya are Siddha Mantras.

Kinds of Mantras

9. There is no Mantra like Gayatri for householders.

10. There is no Mantra like OM for Sannyasins.

11. Guru Mantra is the Mantra given by the Guru.

12. Ishta Mantra is the Mantra of the Devata you worship, your tutelary deity.

13. All Mantras have equal potency or power.

14. Have the Bhava or feeling that Isvara, Devata, Mantra are one.

Mantra's Power

15. There is an indescribable power or Achintya Sakti in the Mantras.

16. The Sakti is the energy of the form of Mantra, i.e., the vibration-forms set up by its sound which carry the man to the Devata that is worshipped.

17. The Mantra-Sakti of the Mantra reinforces the Sadhana-Sakti of the Sadhaka.

18. A Mantra accelerates, generates creative force.

19. Mantra produces harmony in the body and mind.

20. Mantra awakens supernatural powers.

21. The Mantra is awakened from its sleep through the Sadhana-Sakti of the aspirant.

God-realisation Through Mantra

22. Try to realise your unity with the Mantra of the Divinity.

23. Then the Mantra-Sakti will supplement your Sadhana Sakti. Your individual Sakti will be strengthened by the Mantra-Sakti.

24. Mantra is a means of radiant Tejas or energy.

25. If you repeat the Mantra with concentration on its meaning, you will attain God-realisation quickly.

26. Constant repetition of the Mantra with faith, devotion, purity and one-pointed mind awakens the Mantra-chaitanya latent in the Mantra and bestows on the

Sadhaka Mantra-Siddhi, illumination, freedom, peace, eternal bliss and Immortality.

Benefits of Mantra-repetition

27. Mechanical Japa of a Mantra also has its own benefits.

28. The repetition of the Mantra again and again generates great spiritual force and momentum and intensifies the spiritual Samskaras or impressions.

29. Repetition of Surya Mantra bestows health, long life vigour, vitality, Tejas or brilliance, good eyesight, and cures the disease of the eyes.

30. Repetition of Aditya Hridayam in the early morning is highly beneficial. It bestows success, prosperity and illumination.

31. Repetition of Saraswati Mantra—OM Sri Saraswatyai Namah—will bestow wisdom and good intelligence.

32. Repetition of OM Sri Maha Lakshmyai Namah will confer on you wealth.

33. Repetition of Ganesa Mantra—OM Sri Ganesaya Namah—will remove any obstacle in any undertaking and confer wisdom and illumination.

34. Maha Mrityunjaya Mantra will avert accidents, cure incurable diseases and bestow long life and Immortality.

Mantra Initiation

35. Get the Mantra initiation from a Guru.

36. During initiation, the Guru transmits his power to the aspirant.

37. The Kilaka or the pillar supports and makes strong the Mantra.

38. *Hare Rama Hare Rama, Rama Rama Hare Hare; Hare Krishna Hare Krishna, Krishna Krishna Hare Hare.* It

is the Mantra of Kali Santarana Upanishad. Repeat it always.

39. Offer your worship and Japa Sadhana to God Isvararpanamastu, OM Tat Sat Brahmarpanamastu.

40. Mantra Siddhi should not be misused for the destruction of others.

The Mantra Yoga Sadhana

41. Carry on your Sadhana with perseverance and tenacity, without break.

42. It is better to stick to one Mantra alone. See Lord Krishna in Rama, Siva, Durga, Gayatri, etc.

43. Frequent change of Mantra is not beneficial.

44. Gaze at the picture of the Lord for a few minutes and close your eyes. Then try to visualise the picture mentally.

45. The images or thoughts you form in your mind will help you in making what you would become.

46. You can do Japa of a Mantra along with the breath. It is Ajapa Japa.

47. Soham Mantra with the breath is Ajapa Japa. Repeat *So* with inhalation and *Ham* with exhalation.

48. Repeat *Ra* with inhalation and *Ma* with exhalation.

49. Write down daily in a notebook your Ishta Mantra or Guru Mantra for half an hour.

50. Observe Mauna when you write the Mantra.

51. You will have more concentration by this method of Likhita Japa.

52. Live on milk and fruits. Sleep on the floor. Observe Brahmacharya and repeat the Mantra for 40 days continuously. This is Anushthana.

Pada 2

THE GLORY OF THE NAME
Philosophy of Name

53. The glory of the Name of God cannot be established through reasoning or intellect. It can certainly be experienced or realised only through devotion, faith and constant repetition.

54. That which shines above all, having made the whole world equal to a blade of grass, full of the light of consciousness, bliss and purity — it is only the sweet Name of the Lord.

55. Sweeter than all sweet things, more auspicious than all good things, purer than all pure things is the Name of the Lord.

56. OM is everything. OM is the Name of God or Brahman.

57. Name is the bridge that connects the devotee with God.

Name: Its Medicinal Value

58. When all the systems of medicine have failed to cure a disease, divine Namapathy is a sure panacea.

59. God is the One Doctor for all sicknesses. His Name is a potent medicine and tonic.

60. Countless Saktis or mysterious potencies reside in the Lord's Name.

61. Take refuge in the Name. Name and Nami are inseparable.

62. While eating, walking, sitting, recite the Name.

Name: A Means to Moksha

63. God's Name is the Way. Name is the Goal.

64. Name of the Lord is a boat to cross this ocean of Samsara or births and deaths.

65. The Lord resides there at all times where devotees sing Lord's Names with devotion and faith.

66. Name is a weapon to destroy the mind.

67. The sound vibrations of a Mantra or Name generate the image of the Lord of that Mantra and you get the vision of the Lord objectively and subjectively.

The Purifying Power of Name

68. Just as fire has the natural property of burning things, so also the Name of God has the power of burning sins and desires.

69. When you repeat the Mantra, have the feeling that the Lord is seated in your heart, that purity is flowing from the Lord to your mind and that Mantra purifies your heart, destroys your desires, cravings and evil thoughts.

70. The Name serves as a gate-keeper. It never allows worldly thoughts to enter the mind.

71. Man cannot live by bread alone, but he can live on the Name of the Lord.

On the Continuity of Repetition

72. Form a strong habit of repeating the Name of the Lord always.

73. Then alone it will be easy for you to remember Him at the time of death.

74. Nama Smarana or remembrance of the Name should continue throughout the day.

75. The Name of the Lord is the unfailing source of strength in the darkest hour of trial.

76. Give your ears to the hearing, and your speech to the uttering, of Lord's Names. Sing at all times the sweet Names of the Lord.

Mantras for Devotees

77. A devotee of Lord Vishnu should repeat *Om Namo Narayanaya.*

78. A devotee of Lord Siva should do Japa of *Om Namah Sivaya.*

79. A devotee of Lord Krishna should recite *Om Namo Bhagavate Vaasudevaya.*

80. A devotee of Lord Rama should repeat *Om Sri Ramaya Namah.*

81. A devotee of Sri Durga should do Japa of *Om Sri Durgayai Namah.*

Pada 3
JAPA YOGA EXPLAINED
Meaning and Importance of Japa

82. Now then Japa Yoga is explained.

83. Japa is the repetition of any Mantra or Name of the Lord.

84. Japa is the Philosopher's Stone or Divine Elixir that makes one God-like.

85. Lord Krishna says, *"Yajnanam Japayajnosmi."* Among sacrifices I am Japayajna.

86. Japa is the stick in the hands of blind Sadhakas to move on the road to God-realisation.

87. In this Kali Yuga, Japa is the easiest and surest way for God-realisation.

Practice of Japa

88. Do Japa in Brahmamuhurta, 4 a.m. You will derive great benefits.

89. Do the Japa with Nishkama Bhava.

90. Do not beg God for any worldly objects.

---

91. Do Japa of the Mantra or Name with Bhava, feeling, faith and one-pointed mind.

92. Have four sittings for Japa daily, early morning, noon, evening and night.

93. Do Anushtana for 40 days.

94. Do Purascharana. Do one lakh of Japa for each letter. This leads to quick God-realisation.

Instructions on Practice of Japa

95. If you cannot take a bath in the early morning, wash your hands, feet, face and body and sit for doing Japa.

96. Sit on a Kusha grass seat or deer skin or rug. Spread a white cloth over it. This conserves body electricity.

97. Recite prayer before starting to do Japa.

98. Have a steady pose. You must be able to sit on Padma, Siddha, Svastika or Sukha Asana for 3 hours at a stretch.

99. Face the North and the East when you sit for doing Japa.

100. Do not do the Japa in a hurried manner.

101. Pronounce the Mantra distinctly and without mistakes.

102. Do not repeat it too fast or too slow.

103. Use not the index finger while rolling the beads. Use the thumb, the middle and the ring fingers.

104. When counting of the Maala is over, reverse it and come back again Cross not the Meru.

105. Cover your hand with a towel.

106. Be vigilant. Stand up and do the Japa when sleep tries to overpower you.

107. Resolve to finish a definite number of Maalas before leaving the seat.

Mental Japa

108. A Name or Mantra is recited in three ways, viz., verbal or loud utterance (Vaikhari Japa), semi-verbal or humming (Upansu) and mental (Manasic).

109. Mental Japa is more powerful.

110. When the mind becomes steady, do mental Japa.

111. In mental Japa the Name is recited through the mind only. No one can hear it.

112. The fruit of mental Japa is ten thousand times more powerful than that of the other two kinds of Japa.

113. If the mind wanders, do verbal Japa. This will shut out all other external sounds.

Japa Without Maala

114. Maala or rosary is a whip to goad the mind towards God.

115. Sometimes do the Japa without a Maala. Go by the watch.

116. Do Japa with Maala sometimes in the beginning Later on, do mentally. There is some distraction when you count with the Maala.

117. Japa while standing in water is highly beneficial.

118. Japa should become habitual. Even in dreams you must be doing Japa.

119. Regularity in Japa Sadhana is most essential. Sit in the same place and at the same time.

Japa With Meditation

120. Practice of Japa removes the impurities of the mind, destroys sins and brings the devotee face to face with God.

121. Practise meditation along with Japa. This is Japa-Sahita Dhyana (Japa with meditation).

122. Gradually Japa will drop and meditation alone will continue. This is Japa Rahita Dhyana (meditation without Japa).

123. Japa ultimately results in Samadhi or communion with the Lord.

Need for Guru

124. A Guru is necessary for an aspirant.

125. The Guru will remove all obstacles in the spiritual path.

126. Deify your Guru. Do not find defects in him.

127. Guru and God are one.

128. Guru will select your Ishta Devata.

Benefits of Japa

129. Japa induces Vairagya (dispassion).

130. Japa routs out all desires.

131. Japa removes delusion.

132. Japa awakens Kundalini.

133. Japa eradicates all kinds of evil thoughts.

134. Japa transforms the nature of the mind. It fills the mind with Sattva or purity.

135. During Japa all the Divine qualities steadily flow into your mind from the Lord just as oil flows from one vessel to another vessel.

136. Japa changes the mental substance from passion to purity.

137. Japa calms and strengthens the mind.

138. It makes the mind introspective. It checks the outgoing tendencies of the mind.

139. The meditator and the meditated, the worshipper and the worshipped become one and the same. This is Samadhi. This is the fruit of Japa.

Adhyaya Eight

HATHA YOGA SUTRAS

Pada 1

THE PRACTICE OF HATHA YOGA

The Meaning and Place of Hatha Yoga

1. Now then an enquiry into Hatha Yoga.

2. Hatha Yoga means the Yoga of union between *Ha* and *Tha*.

3. Ha means the sun *Tha* means the moon.

4. Prana is known by the name of the sun.

5. Apana is known by the name of the moon.

6. Therefore Hatha Yoga is the union of the Prana and the Apana.

7. Hatha Yoga deals with a system of Yogic exercises of the Indian Rishis and Yogins of yore based on scientific principles.

8. Hatha Yoga is only an auxiliary to Raja Yoga.

9. Raja Yoga begins where Hatha Yoga ends.

Importance of Hatha Yoga

10. Hatha Yoga is a perfectly practical system of Self-culture.

11. Hatha Yoga is a Divine Blessing for attaining good health.

12. Body and mind are the instruments which the practice of Hatha Yoga keeps sound, strong and full of energy.

13. Hatha Yoga imparts to every practitioner fine health, longevity, strength, vim and vitality.

14. Hatha Yoga is a great help to the practice of Raja Yoga.

15. It removes Tamas (inertia) and Rajas (restlessness of the mind and the body).

16. It gives one easy mastery over the turbulent senses.

Qualifications of Yogic Student

17. A student of Hatha Yoga should possess humility, the spirit of selfless service, dispassion, serenity, self-restraint, faith, devotion, honesty truthfulness, non-violence, cosmic love, purity and courage.

18. A Yogic student should take Mithahara — moderate diet. He should take food half stomachful, fill a quarter with water and keep the quarter free for expansion of gas and propitiating the Lord.

19. Brahmacharya (celibacy) is essential for the practice of Hatha Yoga.

20. Keep the mind fully occupied. This is the best panacea for maintaining Brahmacharya.

21. By continence, devotion to Guru, and steady practice for a long time success comes in Yoga after a long time.

Preliminary Instructions

22. Salute to Lord Ganesa and Guru. Recite Guru Stotras before you start the practice.

23. He who is addicted to sensual pleasures, who is arrogant, dishonest, untruthful and who disrespects the Guru is not fit for the practice of Yoga.

24. Unless you are prepared to give up all you have for the service of the Lord and mankind you are not fit for the spiritual path or the path of Yoga.

25. Be regular in your practice. This is most important.

26. Cultivate discrimination, dispassion and a keen desire for attaining emancipation.

27. At the conclusion of practice, offer your Sadhana to the Lord as Isvararpana.

28. Learn the Asanas, Pranayama and Kriyas from a Hatha Yogi Guru. Books also will help you.

29. Recite the Names of the Lord when you practise Asana and Pranayama.

Pada 2

THE YOGIC EXERCISES

The Various Poses

30. Any steady, comfortable pose is Asana.

31. Sirshasana, Oordhva Padmasana are topsy-turvy poses.

32. Paschimottanasana, Yoga Mudra, Maha Mudra, Padahasthasana are forward bending exercises.

33. Dhanurasana, Bhujangasana, Chakrasana, Matsyasana and Supta Vajrasana are backward bending exercises.

34. Ardhamatsyendrasana and Poorna Matsyendrasana are spinal twists.

35. Mayurasana, Salabhasana, Nauli Kriya and Uddiyana Bandha are abdominal exercises.

36. Padmasana, Siddhasana, Svastikasana and Sukhasana are meditative poses.

37. Trikonasana is a sideway bending pose.

38. Savasana is the final relaxing pose.

Aids to Practice of Asanas

39. Practise Yoga Asanas and Pranayama on an empty stomach in the early morning.

40. Practise for 5 or 10 minuets a day, but never miss a day's practice.

41. If you are tired, do Savasana for a few minutes.

42. In Savasana do Japa and meditation. Relax the body and mind completely.

43. There must be joy, invigoration, exhilaration of spirit after the practice.

Benefits of Asanas

44. Practice of Asanas removes diseases and makes the body light, firm and steady.

45. Halasana, Ardha-matsyendrasana and Sarvanga Asana make the spine elastic and make you young.

46. The body comes under your control.

47. Paschimottanasana reduces fat.

48. Bhujanga, Salabha and Dhanura Asanas remove constipation.

49. Paschimottanasana, Vajrasana and Mayurasana help your digestion.

50. Develop thyroid through Sarvangasana.

51. Sirshasana, Sarvangasana and Gorakshasana help to maintain Brahmacharya, and make you an Oordhvareta Yogi.

Pada 3

PRANAS AND PRANAYAMA

The Principle of Energy

52. The Source for Prana is God.

53. Prana is the universal principle of energy or vital force.

54. Breath is the external manifestation of the gross Prana.

55. The seat of Prana is heart.

56. Prana is the vital force. It vibrates and moves the mind.

57. The excess of Prana is stored up in the brain and nervous centres.

58. He who knows Prana knows the Vedas.

The Functions of Prana

59. Prana is expended by thinking, willing, acting, moving, talking, writing, etc.

60. Subtle Prana or psychic Prana generates thinking.

61. Control of Prana leads to control of mind.

62. Gross Prana digests food, pumps blood, excretes and secretes.

63. Prana is supplied by food, water, air and solar energy.

64. The supply of Prana taken up by the nervous system.

65. It is through the power of Prana that the ears hear, the eyes see, and the intellect functions.

66. Prana digests food, excretes and secretes.

The Forms of Prana

67. Prana assumes five forms, viz., Prana, Apana, Samana, Udana and Vyana.

68. The seat of Prana is the heart. The seat of Apana is anus. The seat of Samana is the navel. The seat of Udana is the throat. Vyana is all-pervading.

69. The function of Prana is respiration.

70. Apana does secretion.

71. Samana performs digestion.

72. Udana helps deglutition, swallowing of food. It takes the Jiva to sleep. It separates the astral body from the physical body at the time of death.

73. Vyana performs circulation of blood.

The Five Sub-Pranas

74. Naga, Kurma, Krikara, Devadatta and Dhananjaya are the five sub-Pranas.

75. Naga does eructation and hic-cough.

76. Kurma opens the eyelids.

77. Krikara causes hunger and thirst.

78. Devadatta does yawning.

79. Dhananjaya causes decomposition of the body after death.

The Control of Prana

80. Pranayama is the control of Prana and the vital forces of the body.

81. A correct habit of breathing must be established by the regular practice of Pranayama.

82. Practise Pranayama in a well-ventilated room or upstairs or on the bank of a river or garden. Avoid chill draughts.

83. Do Japa and meditation to begin with at 4 a.m. Then practise Asana and Pranayama.

84. If you want to attain success in Pranayama, you must have steadiness in Asana.

85. Sit on Kusa grass, deer skin and cloth placed one over the other.

86. Repeat Om mentally during Kumbhaka or retention of breath.

87. There should be no suffocation during retention or Kumbhaka.

88. Slowly exhale.

89. Inhalation is Puraka; retention is Kumbhaka; exhalation is Rechaka.

90. If you want to attain Pratyahara, you must know Pranayama well.

Kevala Kumbhaka

91. Kumbhaka or retention of breath bestows longevity.

92. Kevala Kumbhaka is mere retention of breath without inhalation and exhalation.

93. In the beginning, for a few days do only Puraka (inhalation) and Rechaka (exhalation).

94. After some time, combine Kumbhaka (retention) also.

Eight Kinds of Pranayama and Their Results

95. The practice of Pranayama makes the mind fit for concentration.

96. Pranayama sharpens the intellect, develops memory, brain power and the power of concentration.

97. Pranayama removes all diseases and increases the digestive fire and awakens Kundalini Sakti.

98. Suryabheda, Ujjayi, Sitkari, Seetali, Bhastrika, Bhramari, Moorcha, Plavini, are the eight kinds of Pranayama.

99. Bhastrika purifies the Nadis and breaks the three Granthis.

100. Bhastrika strengthens the lungs and cures Asthma and consumption

101. Seetali Pranayama cools your body and purifies the blood.

Pada 4
MUDRAS, BANDHAS, KRIYAS
The Value of Mudras

102. Mudra means a seal. It seals the mind with the Soul or Atman.

103. Mudra does not allow the mind to wander outside towards objects.

104. Mudras concern the mind.

105. Maha Mudra, Yoni Mudra, Yoga Mudra, Khechari Mudra, Vipareeta Karani Mudra, are the important Mudras.

The Work of Bandhas

106. Mulabandha, Jalandharabandha, Uddiyanabandha are the important Bandhas.

107. Bandhas pertain to the Prana. That which binds Prana is Bandha.

108. They do not allow the Prana to move upwards and the Apana to move downwards.

109. They bind and unite the Prana with the Apana and send the united Prana-Apana along the Sushumna Nadi.

110. Mula Bandha helps the Yogic student to take the Apana and the sex-energy upwards by contracting the anus and drawing up the Apana.

111. A combination of Asana, Bandha and Mudra is essential.

The Six Kriyas

112. Dhauti, Basti, Neti, Nauli, Trataka and Kapalabhati are the Shad (six) Kriyas.

113. Shad Kriyas are preliminary purificatory processes.

114. Basti is drawing the water through the anus and letting it out like an enema.

115. Dhauti is cleansing the stomach with a piece of cloth.

116. Nauli is churning of the abdomen.

117. Neti is cleansing the nostrils with a thread.

118. Kapalabhati is a kind of breathing exercise for cleansing the skull.

119. Trataka or gazing develops the power of

concentration to a great degree. It improves eyesight and removes diseases of the eye.

120. Trataka is steadily gazing at a point.

121. Trataka helps concentration of the mind.

Various Purifications

122. Nadi-Suddhi is purification of Nadis.

123. Adhara-Suddhi is purification of Adhara or support.

124. Bhuta-Suddhi is purification of elements.

125. Chitta-Suddhi is purification of mind.

126. Siddhi is not possible without Suddhi.

127. If there is Suddhi (purification), Siddhi (perfection) will come by itself.

Pada 5

NADIS AND CHAKRAS

The Astral Tubes

128. Nadis are astral tubes made up of astral matter that carry Pranic current.

129. Two fingers above the anus and two fingers below the organ of generative is the Kanda.

130. Seventy two thousand Nadis come out of this Kanda.

131. Kanda is the root of all Nadis.

132. Nadis can be seen by the astral eyes only.

133. Of all the Nadis, Sushumna, Ida and Pingala are the most important.

The Three Important Nadis

134. Nadi Suddhi or purification of the Nadis is obtained by the practice of Pranayama.

135. Ida is the Chandra Nadi. It is cool. It flows in the left nostril.

136. Pingala is Surya Nadi. It is hot. It flows in the right nostril.

137. Sushumna stands from the middle of the Kanda to the head.

138. Meditate when the Sushumna Nadi flows through both nostrils. You will have wonderful concentration.

The Centres of Vital Force

139. Chakras are centres of energy or vital force.

140. The Chakras can only be seen by the astral eye.

141. The pineal gland is situated at the Sahasrara.

142. Merudanda is the vertebral column.

143. The pineal gland is the telepathic sense.

The Six Chakras

144. The six Chakras have been identified with the sacro coccygeal plexus, lumbar plexus, solar plexus, laryngeal plexus and cerebellum.

145. Muladhara is a lotus of four petals.

146. Svadhisthana Chakra is a lotus of six petals. It is at the root of the genitals.

147. Manipura Chakra is at the navel. It has 10 petals.

148. Anahata Chakra is the lotus in the heart with 12 petals.

149. Visuddha Chakra is the lotus in the throat with 16 petals.

150. The Ajna Chakra is the lotus in the Trikuti, the space between the two eyebrows. It has two petals.

151. Ajna Chakra is the seat of the mind.

152. Sahasrara Chakra is the thousand-petalled lotus that is located at the crown of the head.

Achievement of the Yogic Student

153. The Yogic student awakens the Kundalini and takes it to the Sahasrara Chakra in the crown of the head.

154. He breaks the Brahma Granthi at Muladhara, Vishnu Granthi at Manipura and Rudra Granthi at Visuddha.

155. The Yogi opens the mouth of Sushumna through Pranayama and takes the Kundalini through the Sushumna to Sahasrara.

156. Sakti is united with Lord Siva at the crown of the head.

Pada 6
GENERAL GUIDANCE AND KUNDALINI
Obstacles in Yoga

157. Disease, langour, doubt, carelessness, the tendency to go after sensual enjoyments, instability, mistaken notions, missing the point are the obstacles in Yoga.

158. Laziness and fickleness of mind are the two great obstacles in Yoga.

159. Too much sleep makes a man dull and lethargic.

160. Sleep for 6 hours is quite sufficient for every individual.

161. If you have ill-feelings towards anyone, remove them.

162. Light, Sattvic diet, Pranayama, Asana will remove laziness.

Important instructions

163. Do not spoil your health in the name of Tapasya.

164. There is no bond equal in strength to Maya and no power greater than Yoga to destroy that bond.

165. Drink a little milk in the end.

166. Wait for one hour for bath.

167. Be moderate in eating and sleeping.

168. Abandon hot curries, chutneys, too much condiments, onions and garlic.

169. Avoid too much of salt, chillies, tamarind, meat, etc.

170. Take milk, ghee, butter, honey, wheat bread, barley, fruits and vegetables.

171. Avoid overwork.

Transmutation of Energy

172. The whole body and all its functions are manifestations of Sakti.

173. When anger is controlled, it will be transmuted into an energy which can move the whole world.

174. When sex energy is sublimated as Ojas, it supplies abundant energy.

175. Be sincere, be earnest, be zealous; you will soon become a great Yogi.

176. Be patient and persevering.

177. Do not take stimulants and narcotics. Draw energy, vitality, inspiration from Pranayama.

Sadhana and Samadhi

178. Salute Lord Ganapati before you begin the practice.

179. The place wherein you can get concentration of mind is suitable for your Yogic practice.

180. Do not stop your Sadhana, when you get some glimpses and experiences.

181. Do not stop your Sadhana when you see visions.

182. Do not think that visions are the highest experience.

183. In the beginning experiences vary in different individuals.

184. If you want to get established in Dhyana or meditation you must know the method of Dharana or concentration.

185. If you want to attain Dharana or concentration you must know perfectly the method of Pratyahara.

186. If you want to attain Samadhi, you must know well the process of Dhyana or meditation.

187. In Samadhi the body is maintained by the nectar which flows from the union of Siva and Sakti in the Sahasrara.

188. When Kundalini operates it helps the Yogic student in the attainment of Nirvikalpa Samadhi or superconscious state.

The Awakening of Kundalini

189. Kundalini can be awakened when a man rises above desires.

190. Kundalini can be awakened by Pranayama, Asanas, Mudras, Bandhas, by concentration, by devotion, by analytical will of the Jnanis, by repetition of Mantras, by the grace of the Guru through touch, sight or mere Sankalpa.

191. No Samadhi is possible without awakening Kundalini and taking it to Sahasrara.

192. Kundalini is the primordial energy that lies in the basal Muladhara Chakra in a dormant potential state.

193. Only a Yogi leading the life of a Brahmachari and observing a moderate and nutritious diet, obtains perfection in the awakening of Kundalini.

194. During the ascent of Kundalini, layer after layer of the mind becomes fully opened.

Fruits of Awakening Kundalini

195. As soon as the Kundalini is awakened, the Yogi gets these six experiences which last for a short time, viz., Ananda (spiritual bliss), Kampan (tremor of the body and limbs), Utthan (rising from the ground), Ghurni (divine intoxication), Murcha (fainting) and Nidra (sleep).

196. The three coils of Kundalini or serpent-power represent Her three Gunas and half coil represents the Vikritis or modifications of the Gunas.

197. At every centre to which the Yogic student rouses the Kundalini, he experiences special forms of bliss and gains special powers.

198. The practitioner of Kundalini Yoga has both Bhukti (enjoyment) and Mukti (liberation).

199. Kundalini Herself, when awakened by the Yogi, achieves for him the Jnana or illumination.

Adhyaya Nine

AROGYA SUTRAS

Pada 1

GOD, PRAYER, HEALTH AND HYGIENE

God: The Source of All Health

1. God is the Source for life, health, energy and happiness.

2. God is the supreme Life-giver, Energiser and Nourisher.

3. Vital Force comes from the One great Source of all life — God.

4. The mysterious human body, the nine-gated city, is the Temple of God. Keep it healthy, pure and strong.

5. The human body is the moving temple of God or the chariot of the Soul.

6. This body should be utilised in the service of God. Keep it quite fit for the service of the Lord and the humanity.

Power of Prayer

7. Meditate ceaselessly on the diseaseless, ever blissful Atman. Chant OM. Sing OM. You will be blessed with immortality, health and happiness.

8. Pray to the Lord just before and after meals.

9. Go to bed by 10 p.m. and get up at 4 a.m. Do some prayer, Japa and meditation.

10. Pray. Do Japa. Sing Lord's Glories. Meditate. You will have wonderful health and eternal happiness.

Achievement of Good Health

11. Health is above wealth and treasure.

12. Health is the state of equilibrium of the three humours of the body; viz., Vatha, Pittha and Kapha (wind, bile and phlegm), wherein the mind and all the organs of the body work in harmony and concord and man enjoys peace and happiness and performs his duties of life with comfort and ease.

13. Good health can be achieved by observing rightly the laws of Health, and the rules of Hygiene, by taking wholesome, light, substantial, easily digestible, nutritious, bland food or Sattvic diet, by inhaling pure air, by regular physical exercise, by daily cold bath and by observing moderation in eating, drinking, etc.

14. Observe the laws and rules of health.

15. For good health, an adult should take 6 glasses of water daily.

16. Good digestion, good assimilation, proper elimination – this is the secret of attaining perfect health and a high standard of health and vitality.

17. He who is moderate in everything, he who basks in the sun, he who takes cold bath in the early morning, he who is ever busy, he who talks a little is healthy and attains long life.

The Philosophy of Health

18. Health alone is truth, not disease.

19. He who has done good deeds in his previous birth enjoys good health in this life.

20. Disease is the result of disobedience of the immutable laws of health that govern life.

21. Every human being is the author of his own health or disease.

22. Good health is very essential for man's success in life and for Yoga Sadhana.

Principles of Health

23. Take care of the stomach. You will keep well.

24. Control your temper and tongue; you will have good health, long life, peace, bliss and prosperity.

25. A fresh and energetic walk in the early morning and evening is very conducive to the maintenance of a high standard of health and vitality for everybody.

26. A real, sharp, good hunger is a sign of good, radiant health.

27. Sudden changes in the regimen of diet are disastrous to health and should be depreciated.

28. Alcohol is an enemy of health. Shun it absolutely.

29. Drugging must be avoided. It spoils health.

30. He who is endowed with sufficient vital force enjoys good health.

31. Physical exercise, proper rest, pure air, proper ventilation, sunlight, clean body, cheerfulness and contentment, healthful dress, proper diet, healthful working, regularity in eating, avoidance of stimulants and narcotics are the essential principles of health.

Hints on Hygiene

32. Try to acquire at least an elementary knowledge in sanitation, hygiene, the nature and uses of common Home Remedies, the nature and treatment of common diseases and first-aid to the injured.

33. Hygiene is the art of preserving health. It aims at rendering growth more perfect, decay less rapid, life more vigorous, and death more remote.

34. Keep the mouth very, very clean. Remove the tartar.

35. Rinse the mouth nicely with luke warm salt water at the end of each meal and tiffin.

36. Keep the mouth and teeth always clean. Wash them well after every meal.

37. Do not eat sweetmeats of the bazaar during cholera season.

38. Do not use another man's cloth.

39. Do not sleep in another man's bedding.

40. The habit of always remaining in suits and boots is highly deleterious to health. Give up tight collars.

41. Pare your nails close and keep them quite clean.

Pada 2

NATURE CURE, MENTAL HEALTH, YOGIC EXERCISES

Elements of Nature Cure

42. Nature cure is both a therapy and a way of life.

43. Nature itself is your best guide.

44. Live with nature. Use herbs and greens. Avail yourself of the healing agencies of nature in the sun, air, water, earth, herbs and fasting, etc.

45. Sleep is nature's tonic for a healthy life.

46. Sunlight is a cheap and universal tonic and wonderful disinfectant.

47. Sun-bath has wonderful effect. It replenishes vitamin 'D'.

48. Walk. Never run upstairs.

49. Diarrhoea is a self-cleansing effort of Nature. It is unwise to stop at once diarrhoea by astringents and opiates.

50. Pure air is the best of all tonics.

51. Lead a life in tune with nature.

52. A return to natural life is the first step to recovery.

Roads to Mental Health

53. Good mental health can be attained by Japa, meditation, Brahmacharya, practice of Yama, Niyama, right conduct, right thinking, right feeling, right speaking and right action, Atma Vichara, relaxation of mind and practice of cheerfulness, and Pranayama.

54. Selfishness, greed, lust, anger, hatred, jealousy, fear, worry destroy mental health.

55. Cheerfulness is the best tonic.

56. Have a calm and poised mind. You will enjoy wonderful physical and mental health.

57. Mind is the cause of the making of this body of ours.

58. Mental health is most important than physical health.

Yogic Exercises

59. Sit on Vajrasana after every meal. This helps digestion. Sit on Vajrasana for 10 minutes.

60. Deep breathing and Pranayama strengthen the lungs and remove various diseases.

61. Regular practice of Yogic exercises, or Yoga Asanas, even for 15 minutes a day, will keep you quite fit; you will have abundant energy, muscular strength and nerve power, a charming personality and will live long.

62. Brahmacharya is a help to attain your health and long life. Therefore observe Brahmacharya.

63. Brahmacharya, prayer, meditation, Pranayama, Sattvic food augment the vital force and bestow good health, vim, vigour and vitality.

Pada 3

FASTING, FRUITS AND FOOD

Importance of Fasting

64. Fasting causes rejuvenation of tissues, gives rest to the organs, increases elimination, improves the power of digestion and assimilation and causes absorption of abnormal growths.

65. Fasting is a therapeutic of the highest degree.

66. Instead of using medicine better fast a day.

67. Fasting is nature's greatest curative agent. It can restore health when everything else has failed.

68. Fasting increases elimination of toxins.

69. Fasting is the most efficient means of correcting any disease.

70. Fasting increases the assimilating powers of the body.

71. Fasting is useful in appendicitis, diabetes, epilepsy, piles, high blood pressure.

72. Fasting eliminates poison from the system and removes many diseases.

73. Fasting is the greatest remedy.

74. Fast and give abundant rest to the digestive organs.

Value of Fruit-Diet

75. Purify the blood by taking fresh fruits such as grapes, oranges, pomegranates and mosambies.

76. Fruit-juice supplies abundant energy in a short time.

77. Live on juicy fruits for a week. This will eliminate impurities from the system.

78. Lemon-juice cures scurvy. It is an important article of diet.

79. Fruits which leave residues or vegetables should not be given in typhoid.

80. Spinach and tomatoes contain iron. They are beneficial in anaemic patients.

81. Torpidity of liver is removed by eating tomatoes which contain calomel.

82. Tomato is both a blood-forming and blood-purifying vegetable.

83. If you wish to attain longevity and good health, live on milk and fruits.

84. Take fruit-diet when you meditate vigorously.

85. Papaya contains papain. It helps digestion.

86. Orange-juice is very invigorating and vitalising.

Guidance on Food

87. Food is the form of Lord. Energy is the essence of food. Mind is the essence of energy. Knowledge is the essence of mind. Bliss is the essence of Knowledge.

88. Do not allow flies to sit on food. Flies are carriers of cholera, typhoid and dysentery.

89. Wrong feeding is the main cause of disease.

90. Take only a light meal at night. This will give you sound sleep.

91. Never heat the food again over the fire.

92. Take food as medicine. Give up gluttony.

93. Improper food causes accumulation of waste matter which poisons the system.

94. Take a well-balanced diet.

95. Whatever food you eat and air you breathe serve to create and rejuvenate your blood.

96. Food serves as fuel for our body-engine and supplies animal heat and vital energy.

97. The body is built from food by the medium of blood.

98. Food must contain proteins, fat, carbohydrates and minerals in proper quantity. Vitamin A, B, C, D, etc., must also be there.

Food and Health

99. The secret of being always healthy and happy is to be a little hungry all the time.

100. A simple diet is conducive to health and long life.

101. Have a restricted diet on Sundays. Take an all-fruit diet on Mondays. Live on milk diet on Tuesdays.

102. Never take food in a hurry.

103. Quality of food is more important than quantity.

104. Do not eat anything between two meals.

105. Follow the rules of common sense. If you have found out that a certain article of diet absolutely disagrees with you, abstain from it.

Specific Diet for Diseases

106. Take starch-sugar-free diet in diabetes.

107. A Rice diet is beneficial in blood-pressure.

108. Take salt-free diet in diseases of the kidney.

109. In typhoid the most essential thing is diet.

110. Take fat-free diet in diseases of the liver.

111. Take tamarind-free diet in fevers.

112. Take chilli-free diet in diarrhoea and dysentery.

113. Take always sour, oil, chilli, jaggery, onion, garlic free diet.

114. Plain food eaten at regular hours is of the greatest importance in all forms of indigestion.

115. Beans, peas, lettuce, spinach, cabbages are body-building and repairing foods.

116. Give up meat, fish, eggs, etc. They excite the passions and produce diseases.

117. Do not take tinned foods and old butter.

118. Brown bread produces strong bones and better teeth in the young.

119. Asthmatics should not take any food after 3 p.m. The last meal should be light.

120. If an article of food disagrees, reduce the quantity rather than forbid it entirely.

121. Avoid rich foods, unnatural foods, overloading or stuffing the stomach.

122. Milk is a perfect food. It contains all constituents of diet in perfect proportion.

INSTRUCTIONS ON PRESERVATION OF HEALTH

Pada 1

Theses on Eating

123. Do not eat anything which you do not like, but do not eat everything which you like most.

124. Do not eat when you are angry.

125. Eat when you are hungry.

126. Eat to live and not live to eat.

127. Avoid late dinners.

128. Eat only combinations that are compatible.

129. Observe silence when you take your food.

130. Do not overload the stomach. Eat moderately.

131. Avoid too cold or too hot food or drinks.

132. Avoid excess of all sorts.

133. Masticate every morsel of food thoroughly.

134. Do not take too many dishes.

135. Avoid overeating, which is the cause for most of the diseases.

136. Never work hard within half an hour after eating.

137. Eat curry of plantain-stem. This will dissolve stones in the kidneys and the bladder.

138. Lead a well-regulated life.

139. Regularity in the hours of meals is very necessary.

Pada 2
Cure for Constipation

140. Constipation is the cause for many diseases. Combat against it successfully.

141. Figs and prunes are beneficial in constipation.

142. Remove constipation. You will have no piles.

143. A glass of lukewarm water at night and in the early morning is beneficial in constipation.

144. Effort should be always made to overcome constipation by diet, and other simple means rather than by constantly taking purgatives or using enema.

145. For constipation myrobalan may be taken at night before going to bed. This does not create a drug habit. It is useful to the system in various other ways too.

146. He who suffers from constipation must take plenty of vegetables and fruits.

147. Whole-meal bread, porridge, tomatoes, celery, oranges, apples, stewed prunes, melons, figs are all useful in constipation.

Pada 3
Vegetables

148. Take spinach, tomatoes, grapes in anaemia, as they contain much iron.

149. Do not remove the skin of apples or carrots. They contain valuable minerals and vitamins.

150. Carrots are blood-forming vegetables.

151. Fresh lime-juice is a blood restorative and preservative *par excellence*.

152. The juice of a small lemon, spinach, one or two tomatoes, a little fresh cocoanut, bananas, green gram sprouts, half a seer of milk, two teaspoonfuls of honey, can give you wonderful health, vigour, vitality and longevity.

153. Take lemon-juice and honey as the first thing in the morning.

154. He who drinks butter-milk, eats tomatoes, takes lemon and honey in the early morning, and walks three miles daily is healthy and attains longevity.

155. Give up morning tiffin or morning breakfast. Take a cup of milk with a tablespoonful of honey in the early morning.

Pada 4
Air and Water

156. Fresh pure air is the finest circulatory tonic.

157. Open air life is an infallible cure for consumption.

158. Take water a few minutes after you have finished your meals.

159. Drink a tumbler of cold or lukewarm water in the early morning as soon as you get up from the bed (Usha Pana). This will flush the kidneys and give a good movement of bowels.

160. Do not throw away the water in which wheat, rice and vegetables have been boiled. Drink it. The water contains valuable minerals.

161. Barley water is a refreshing and cooling beverage in fevers, diarrhoea, dysentery, diseases of the kidneys and in burning sensation of the urine.

162. Give barley-water in abundance in renal colic.

Pada 5

Milk and Butter-Milk

163. Milk is the richest source of calcium. Cheese is next.

164. Indigestion arising from eating mangoes is cured by drinking milk.

165. Take butter-milk, spinach and tomatoes and plenty of fruits.

166. Butter-milk contains lactic acid. It helps digestion. It is useful in diarrhoea, dyspepsia and dysentery. It is a cooling and refreshing drink. It destroys intestinal germs. It is nutritious.

167. He who drinks butter-milk, he who eats tomatoes, spinach and lemons, he who walks three miles daily is healthy and attains long life.

Important Instructions

168. The prospective mother should not listen to the old women who talk on the pains and perils of child birth.

169. Heart, lungs and brain are the tripods of life.

170. Regulate your activities, so that no greater demand on the heart is made at any moment than it is capable of meeting.

171. Get up from the table when you are still hungry.

172. Excessive fat, overloading the stomach, putting off answering the nature's call, immoderate drink, sleep by day and wake by night – these are the causes of illness.

173. Hunger is a call for food. It is really a call for blood.

174. The heart is the central organ of the circulatory system. It pumps blood.

175. Attention should always be paid to the wishes and tastes of the patient.

176. Do not allow your babies to be kissed at the lips. Syphilis, consumption, etc. may be communicated to the innocent children.

177. No drastic or irritative purgative should be given to a pregnant woman. Castor oil is beneficial.

178. Practise for a few days to live without salt and sugar.

179. Do not bathe within two hours of meal, when tired after physical exercises, when the body is profusely perspiring or when the body is very warm, when the stomach is loaded with food.

180. Abandon too many mixtures or combination in your diet. It is difficult for the digestive juices to digest complex, diverse combinations.

181. There should be six hours of sleep for a man. Sleep on your left side at night. This will help quick digestion.

182. Proteins, mineral salts, vitamins and water are the body-builders.

183. Vitamins are life-giving substances.

Removal of Diseases

184. Uric acid and urea are removed by fasting.

185. Rheumatism is cured by sun-bath and steam bath.

186. Proper elimination is as important as a correct diet. You must have a good motion daily in the early morning.

187. Indigestion caused by the excessive use of ghee is removed by lemon-juice.

188. Endeavour to qualify yourself as your own doctor.

189. Pears are beneficial in stones in the bladder or kidneys. It dissolves the stones

190. Empty your bladder and bowels before you go to bed.

191. Carbohydrates and fats are energy-producers. They serve as fuel.

Mind As a Source of Disease

192. Diseases take their origin in the mind (Adhi)

193. Give up imaginary fear of diseases. Fear havocs more than the disease itself.

194. Disease is lack of ease.

195. Give up false imagination. Blood pressure has caused even healthy persons to worry about imaginary blood-pressure and to get into thereby the condition of that they dreaded most.

196. Nip the malady in the bud. Do not allow it to strike deep roots.

197. Pessimistic thoughts, fear of diseases, lack of proper food, overworking late at night, various kinds of anxieties and worries impair good health.

198. *Dharmartha kama mokshanam arogyam moolamuttamam: Rogasthasya apahartare sreyaso jivitayacha.* Health is the best cause of virtue. Wealth, enjoyment and emancipation is the blessedness of life. Diseases are the destroyers of health.

199. *Sariram Adyam Khalu Dharma Sadhanam.* Body is indeed the foremost essential thing for the attainment of the goal of human existence.

TANTRA YOGA SUTRAS

Pada 1

TANTRA YOGA SASTRA

Accents of Tantra Yoga

1. Now then an enquiry into Tantra Yoga.

2. Tantra is so called because it explains (Tanoti) in great detail knowledge concerning Tattva (Truth) and because it saves (Tranat).

3. Tantra Yoga is a Gupta Vidya.

4. Tantra Yoga should be learnt from a Guru.

5. Tantra Yoga lays special emphasis on the development of the power latent in the six Chakras, from Muladhara to Ajna.

6. Tantra is the saving Knowledge, the raft which carries the Sadhaka safely to the port of Freedom or Emancipation.

7. You will have to get the knowledge and practice from the Tantra Gurus who hold the key to it.

Spiritual Practices in Tantra

8. Tantra Sadhana bestows tremendous Siddhis or powers.

9. Tantras are Sadhana Sastras, the teaching about the path to perfection.

10. Sadhana means any spiritual practice that helps the aspirant to realise God.

11. Worship, meditation, service of Guru, study of

scriptures, Tapas and the Pancha Tattva Mantra, are means
to attain realisation of Mother.

12. The qualifications of the disciple are purity, faith,
devotion, dispassion, truthfulness and control of the
senses.

13. Tapas is penance or austerity.

14. Real Tapas is concentration and meditation.

15. Sattvic Tapas or practice without desire for fruit is
the best.

16. The Sadhaka shines with spiritual effulgence by the
practice of Tapas.

17. Vrata is the performance for the purification of the
mind.

Attainment of Siddhis

18. Siddhi is perfection or realisation.

19. Siddha is one who has attained perfection.

20. Siddhi is attained by Sadhana. Sadhaka is one who
practises Sadhana.

21. Bhuta Siddhi is an important Tantrik rite. It is
purification of the five elements of which the body is
composed.

22. The Sadhaka infuses into the body the life of Devi
by this purification.

23. Do not run after Siddhis or psychic powers. You will
get a downfall.

24. One may attain Siddhi in speech, Siddhi in Mantra,
Siddhi in Yoga, etc.

Nyasa, Yantra, Mudra

25. Nyasa is a very important and powerful Tantrik rite.

26. Nyasa is placing the tips of the fingers of the right
hand on various parts of the body, accompanied by Mantra.

27. Yantra takes the place of image. It is an object of worship in Tantra Yoga.

28. Yantra is a diagram. It is the body of the Devata.

29. It is engraved on a metal. The Devata is installed in the Yantra.

30. The one Brahman is invoked by different names, in order to protect the different parts of the body. This is Kavacha.

31. Mudra is ritual of manual gestures. This gives pleasure to Devatas.

Pada 2
PRACTICAL PHILOSOPHY OF THE SAKTAS

The Sakti Treatises

32. The Sakti philosophy is as old as the Vedas.

33. The Saktas accept the Vedas as the basic scriptures and the Sakta Tantras as texts expounding the means to attain the goal set forth in the Vedas.

34. The Sakti Tantra is Advaita Veda. It proclaims that Paramatman and Jivatman are one.

35. The Devi Sukta in the Rig Veda is the real source of the Sakti doctrine.

36. The glory of the Devi is sung in the Sakta Agamas and Tantras and in the Devi Bhagavatam also.

The Worship of Sakti

37. Universe is power. Universe is a manifestation of Devi's glory.

38. Sakti worship is worship of God's glory, of God's greatness and supremacy.

39. Mother is manifest in all beings as Vak. She is Vaksakti (power of Speech).

40. Sakti binds the individual soul through the power of Avidya or ignorance.

41. She releases him through the power of Vidya or wisdom.

Forms of Sakti Worship

42. Offer Asana, Arghya, Padya, Achamana, bathing, dressing, ornaments, scents, flowers, lights, etc., to Devi. This is external worship.

43. Worship the Devi in the internal Chakras. This is internal worship.

44. Worship Devi with devotion intensely during Navaratri. Live on milk and fruits and observe celibacy. Study Durga Sapta Sati.

45. Do Chandi Havan. Feed 9 Kanyas.

46. Mother-worship is the worship of God as the Divine Mother — Sri Mata.

47. Pancha Tattva is essential for the worship of Sakti.

Forms of Sakti

48. Worship the Mother in all Her manifestations.

49. Durga, Kaali, Bhagavati, Bhavani, Ambal, Ambika, Jagadambal, Kameswari, Ganga, Uma, Chandi, Chamundi, Lalita, Gauri, Kundalini, Tara, Rajeswari, Tripurasundari, etc., are all Her Forms.

50. Radha, Durga, Lakshmi, Saraswati and Savitri are the five Prakritis.

51. Sakti is symbolic female; but it is in reality neither male nor female but only a force which manifests itself in various forms.

52. Sakti in relation to the three functions of creation, preservation and destruction is Saraswati, Lakshmi and Kaali.

53. Saraswati is cosmic intelligence, cosmic consciousness and cosmic Knowledge.

54. Lakshmi is material wealth and all kinds of prosperity, glory, magnificence, exaltation or greatness.

Bija Akshara and Mantras

55. A Bija Akshara is a seed letter. It is very powerful.

56. Every Devata has his or her own Bija Akshara.

57. Hrim is the Bijakshara of Maya.

58. Aim is the Bijakshara of Saraswati.

59. Sreem is the Bijakshara of Mahalakshmi.

60. Devi Mantras are Om Sri Durgayai Namah, Om Sri Kaalikayai Namah, Om Sri Maha Lakshmyai Namah and Om Sri Saraswatyai Namah.

Chakra Pooja

61. In Chakra Pooja, the worshippers sit in a circle, men and women alternately.

62. The Sakti sits on the left side of the Sadhaka.

63. The Lord of the Chakra sits with his Sakti in the centre.

64. Do Manasic Pooja. This is more powerful than external worship.

65. Pure consciousness is Siva.

66. The same Reality in the Creative Force is Sakti.

67. Without Sakti the phenomenal world cannot be.

68. Without Purusha or Siva, true knowledge cannot be attained.

70. Therefore both should be worshipped — the Maha Kaali and the Mahakaala.

Pada 3

THE DIVINE MOTHER
Nature of the Mother

71. Salutations to the Mother, Adi-Parasakti, who is the Creatrix and Nourisher of the universe!

72. The Mother is a mysterious, indescribable Power of the Supreme Being.

73. She is the dynamic aspect of the Supreme, transcendental Being.

74. The Mother sees through your eyes, hears through your ears and works through your hands.

75. Worship of the Universal Mother leads to attainment of Knowledge of the Self.

Siva and Sakti

76. Siva is the supreme, unchanging Consciousness and Sakti is the Kinetic Power.

77. The word "Sakti" comes from the root "Sak" which means to be able "to do".

78. Sakti in its Static state is Chit-Sakti and in its Kinetic State it is Maya Sakti.

79. Sakti is the creative aspect of the Absolute.

80. She is symbolised as Cosmic Energy.

81. The body, mind, Prana and intellect and all their functions are the Manifestations of the Mother.

82. Mother is Adi Sakti, Para Sakti, Maha Sakti and Chit Sakti.

83. Devi is synonymous with Sakti or the Divine Power that manifests and sustains the universe.

84. God and Sakti are like fire and heat of fire.

Sri Vidya

85. Sri Vidya is the great Mantra of Tripurasundari.

86. It is also called the Panchadasakshari for it is formed of 15 letters.

87. In its developed form it consists of 16 letters, Shodasakshari.

88. Get the initiation from a Guru who has got Siddhi of this Mantra.

89. Worship of Sri Vidya will bestow all powers and Moksha.

Diksha and Sattvic Man

90. Diksha is the giving of Mantra by the Guru.

91. There is no difference between the Guru, Mantra and Devata.

92. Study Sapta Sati or Devi Mahatmya and Lalita Sahasranama, Ananda Lahari, Saundarya Lahari.

93. A Tamasic man has Pasu Bhava.

94. A Rajasic man has Veera Bhava.

95. A Sattvic man has Divya Bhava.

Grace of the Mother

96. Mother's Grace is boundless. Her Mercy is illimitable.

97. Mother will transform your entire life, and bless you with the milk of wisdom, spiritual insight and Kaivalya.

98. Mother gives you Bhukti (material prosperity) and Mukti (liberation).

99. The Devi not only the principle of Creation, the principle of auspiciousness, the principle of cosmic energy, but is also the principle of Divine Knowledge.

100. Power (Sakti) and possessor of Power, Sakta, are not different.

101. The Grace of the Mother is an indispensable factor to attain Moksha or emancipation.

102. Sing Mother's praise; recite Her Names. Worship Her with faith and devotion.

103. Make a total, unreserved, ungrudging surrender to Her. She will bless you.

NADA YOGA SUTRAS

Pada 1
THE SCIENCE OF SPIRITUAL SOUND
Definition of Nada Yoga

1. Now then an enquiry into Nada Yoga.

2. Nada is sound.

3. Sound is vibration.

4. Nada is Siva Sakti.

5. Sakti Tattva becomes for the first time active as Nada.

6. Nada Yoga is called Laya Yoga.

7. Kundalini Yoga is also called Laya Yoga.

8. There is no Laya like Nada.

History of Nada

9. Brahman willed. There was Satsankalpa. A vibration or *Spandana* arose. There was vibration of Om. This is Nada.

10. Nada is that aspect of Sakti which evolves into Bindu.

11. The union and mutual relation of Siva and Sakti is Nada.

12. Sakti Tattva becomes for the first time active as Nada.

13. From Nada comes Maha Bindu.

14. Nada develops into Bindu.

15. Nada and Bindu exist in all Bija Mantras.

16. Nada is the first emanation-stage in the production of Mantra.

17. The second is Bindu.

Nada: The Subtle Aspect of Sound

18. Nada is action.

19. Nada is not the gross sound which is heard by the ear.

20. Nada is the most subtle aspect of Sabda.

21. By one who is desirous of attaining perfection in Yoga Nada alone must be heard and mediated upon with a calm mind, having abandoned all thoughts.

Pre-requisites of Nada Yoga Sadhana

22. Enquiry into the mystic sounds is Nada-Anusandhana.

23. Nadanusandhana means meditation on Nada or sound that is heard at the Anahata Chakra.

24. The essential pre-requisites for Nada Yoga Sadhana are the same as those for any other Yoga Sadhana.

25. Ethical and moral virtues are the first important pre-requites.

Nadopasana

26. Sangeeta or music is the best form of Nadopasana. Sangeeta is identical with God.

27. Nadopasana becomes Nadasvaroopa or God.

28. Nadopasana itself bestows Advaitic realisation on the Sadhaka.

29. Brahman is incomprehensible in its transcendental aspect. The nearest approach it is only Sound or Apara Brahman or Sabda Brahman.

Pada 2

THE MYSTERIES OF SOUND

The Status of Sound

30. Sound is the first manifestation of the Absolute.

31. Sound is the basis of all creation.

32. Therefore it has the power to absorb the other manifestations.

33. Sound has the power to attract and absorb the mind.

Gradations of Sound

34. Sounds are vibrations. They give rise to different forms.

35. Para, Pasyanti, Madhyama and Vaikhari are the various gradations of sound.

36. In Para the sound remains in an undifferentiated form.

37. The seat of Madhyama is the heart.

38. The seat of Pasyanti is navel, or the Manipura Chakra.

39. The seat of Vaikhari is in the throat and mouth.

The Ten Anahata Sounds

40. Sit on Padmasana or Sukhasana. Close the ears with the thumbs through Yoni Mudra. You will hear ten kinds of Anahata sounds.

41. The sound that you hear will make you deaf to all external sounds.

42. The first sound is Chini.

43. The second is Chin-chini.

44. The third is the sound of bell.

45. The fourth is like that of a conch.

46. The fifth is like that of lute.

47. The sixth is like that of a cymbal.

48. The seventh is like that of a flute.

49. The eighth is like that of a drum.

50. The ninth is like that of a Mridanga.

51. The tenth is like that of a thunder.

Meaning of Anahata

52. Anahata sound is not the result of striking or beating certain things, like the raising of a note on the violin or the Veena.

53. Anahata literally means unbeaten, unstruck.

54. Anahata sounds are heard with or without closing the ears.

55. Anahata sound is caused by the vibration of Prana in the heart.

Relation of Mind to Sound

56. Mind is naturally attracted by sweet sounds.

57. It is entrapped by the sweet sounds, just as a deer is entrapped by sweet music.

58. When the mind is attracted by sweet sounds, it forgets all about the sensual objects.

59. When the mind is absorbed in sound it does not run after sensual objects.

60. Melodious sound helps the control of the mind easily.

Pada 3
Sadhana for Mind-control

61. Practise Yama or self-restraint. Control your passion. Cultivate dispassion. Abandon all worldly thoughts. Concentrate on the Anahata sound which annihilates the mind.

62. Practise Prahayama. Do Ajapa-mantra of Soham. You will hear the sounds audibly in a short time.

63. The beating of a drum, the roar of thunder is a Dhvani. There is no manifestation of letters here (unlettered sound).

64. Letters or Varnas are manifested in the case of sounds of articulated speech. This is Varnatmaka Sabda (uttered speech).

Pada 4

Experience in Nada Yoga

65. Hear the sounds through the right ear.

66. Change your concentration from the gross sound to the subtle. The mind will soon be absorbed in sound.

67. You will get knowledge of hidden things when you hear the seventh.

68. You will hear Para-vak when you hear the eighth sound.

69. You will develop divine eye — the eye of intuition — when you hear the ninth.

70. You may experience the tenth sound without the first nine sounds through the initiation of a Guru.

71. The sound entraps the mind. The mind becomes one with the sound as the milk with water.

72. The mind becomes absorbed in Brahman or the Absolute (Laya or dissolution).

73. You will attain the seat of eternal bliss.

74. You will enter into Samadhi and attain Knowledge of the Self.

GURU BHAKTI YOGA

1. The Limbs of Guru Bhakti Yoga
2. The Aim of Guru Bhakti Yoga
3. Principle of Guru Bhakti Yoga
4. Guru Bhakti Yoga as a Science
5. Fruits of Guru Bhakti Yoga
6. Sadhana of Guru Bhakti Yoga
7. Importance of Guru Bhakti Yoga
8. Stumbling Blocks on the Path
9. Fundamentals of Guru Bhakti Yoga
10. Cardinal Notes in Guru Bhakti Yoga
11. Pathway to Immortal Bliss
12. Greatness of Guru Bhakti Yoga
13. Instructions to the Students

The Limbs of Guru Bhakti Yoga

1. Now then an exposition of Guru Bhakti Yoga.

2. Guru Bhakti Yoga is total self-surrender to Sadguru.

3. The important eight limbs of the Guru Bhakti Yoga are viz., (a) the real lasting aspiration to practise Guru Bhakti Yoga; (b) absolute faith in the thoughts, words and actions of Sadguru; (c) doing Sashtanga Namaskara with humility and repeating Guru's name; (d) perfect obedience in carrying out Guru's commands; (e) doing personal service to Sadguru without expectation of fruits; (f) daily worshipping of the lotus-feet of Sadguru with Bhava and devotion; (g) self-surrender or dedication of Thanu, Manas and Dhana in the cause of divine mission of Sadguru; (h)

meditation on the holy feet of Sadguru for obtaining his benign grace; and hearing his holy Upadesa and sincerely practising it.

4. Guru Bhakti Yoga is a Yoga by itself.

5. It is not possible for an aspirant to enter the spiritual path that leads to the union with God unless he practises Guru Bhakti Yoga.

6. He who understands the system of Guru Bhakti Yoga Philosophy can only surrender to his Guru unconditionally.

7. The highest object of life, i.e., Self-realisation is achieved through the practice of Guru Bhakti Yoga.

8. Yoga of Guru Bhakti is the real safe Yoga which can be practised without any fear.

9. The essence of Guru Bhakti Yoga lies in utter obedience in carrying out the Guru's orders and translating his teachings in life.

The Aim of Guru Bhakti Yoga

10. The aim of Guru Bhakti Yoga is to free man from the thraldom of matter and fetters of Prakriti and make him realise his absolute independent nature, through complete surrender to Guru.

11. He who practises the Yoga of Guru Bhakti can annihilate the egoism without any difficulty and he can very easily cross the quagmire of Samsara.

12. Guru Bhakti Yoga bestows immortality and eternal bliss on one who practises it sincerely and regularly.

13. Practice of Guru Bhakti Yoga gives peace and steadiness of mind; it is the master-key to open the realm of elysian bliss.

14. The goal of life is to obtain the benign grace of Sadguru by practising Guru Bhakti Yoga.

Principles of Guru Bhakti Yoga

15. With humility approach the adorable feet of Sadguru. Do prostrations to the life-saving feet of Sadguru. Take shelter under the lotus-feet of Sadguru. Worship the sacred feet of Sadguru. Meditate on the holy feet of Sadguru. Offer the valuable gifts on the sanctifying feet of Sadguru. Dedicate your life to the service of glorious feet of Sadguru. Become the dust of the divine feet of Sadguru. This is the secret of Guru Bhakti Yoga.

16. Self-surrender to the sacred feet of Sadguru is the very foundation of Guru Bhakti Yoga.

17. All that is wanted of you is sincere and earnest effort in the path of Guru Bhakti Yoga.

18. Devotion to Guru is the greatest factor in the practice of Guru Bhakti Yoga.

19. Faith in the Guru is the first rung in the ladder of Guru Bhakti Yoga.

20. The cream of the Guru Bhakti Yoga is absolute (blind) faith in the thoughts, words and actions of the Brahma Nishta Guru who is well-versed in the sacred scriptures.

Guru Bhakti Yoga As a Science

21. The highest and the easiest Yoga to practise in this age is Yoga of Guru Bhakti.

22. The greatest point in the philosophy of Guru Bhakti Yoga is to identify the Guru with the Absolute.

23. The practical aspects of philosophy of Guru Bhakti Yoga is to realise the oneness of Guru with his Istha Devata.

24. Guru Bhakti Yoga is not a system which can be taught by lectures or correspondence courses. The student should live under a preceptor for many years and lead a

rigorous life of austerity, discipline, celibacy and practice of deep meditation.

25. Guru Bhakti Yoga is the science of all sciences.

Fruits of Guru Bhakti Yoga

26. Guru Bhakti Yoga confers immortality, eternal bliss, freedom, perfection, perennial joy, and everlasting peace.

27. The practice of Guru Bhakti Yoga induces non-attachment and dispassion for worldly objects and bestows Kaivalya Moksha.

28. The practice of Guru Bhakti Yoga will help the disciple to control the emotions and passions and will give him power to resist temptations and to remove the disturbing elements from the mind and make him fit to receive Guru's Grace which takes him to the other shore of darkness.

29. Practice of Guru Bhakti Yoga bestows immortality, supreme peace and perennial joy.

30. The practice of Guru Bhakti Yoga will enable you to get rid of fear, ignorance, pessimism, confusion of mind, disease, despair, worry, etc.

Sadhana of Guru Bhakti Yoga

31. Guru Bhakti Yoga is the transformation of the ego-sense which consists in transmutation of individual feeling, willing, understanding, determining into infinite Consciousness.

32. The Sadhanas laid down in the Guru Bhakti Yoga are very simple and sure ways to take to the other shore of fearlessness.

33. Guru Bhakti Yoga is a method of strict discipline achieved through the grace of Guru.

34. Service of Guru without expectation of fruits and ever-increasing devotion to the lotus-feet of Guru is the

integral Sadhana according to the Guru Bhakti Yoga system of philosophy.

35. He who practises Guru Bhakti Yoga without ethical perfection, devotion to Guru, etc., cannot obtain the grace of Guru.

Importance of Guru Bhakti Yoga

36. Guru Bhakti Yoga is the foundation of all other Yogas, viz., Karma Yoga, Bhakti Yoga, Raja Yoga, Hatha Yoga, etc.

37. He who has turned his face from the path of Guru Bhakti Yoga goes from death to death, from darkness to darkness and ignorance to ignorance.

38. Practice of Guru Bhakti Yoga offers a clear definite path for the realisation of the highest end of life.

39. Practice of Guru Bhakti Yoga is open to one and all.

40. All great souls, all master-minds have done great work through the practice of Guru Bhakti Yoga.

41. Guru Bhakti Yoga includes all other Yogas. Without taking recourse to Guru Bhakti Yoga nobody can practise other Yogas which are hard to tread.

42. Guru Bhakti Yoga school of thought gives great importance to obtaining Guru Kripa through Acharyopasana.

43. Guru Bhakti Yoga is as old as Vedic and Upanishadic time.

44. Guru Bhakti Yoga teaches the way to wipe out all pains and sorrows in life.

45. Guru Bhakti Yoga is the only unfailing remedy for the ills of life.

46. The path of Guru Bhakti Yoga brings fruits quickly only for a worthy disciple.

47. Guru Bhakti Yoga ends in the annihilation of ego and attainment of bliss Immortal.

48. Guru Bhakti Yoga is the best Yoga.

Stumbling Blocks on the Path

49. Shyness to do Sashtanga prostration to the sacred feet of Guru is a great hindrance in the practice of Guru Bhakti Yoga.

50. Self-sufficiency, self-justification, vanity, self-conceit, self-assertion, procrastination, obstinacy, fault-finding, evil company, dishonesty, arrogance, lust, anger, greed, and egoism are the great stumbling blocks on the path of Guru Bhakti Yoga.

51. Annihilate the fluctuating potency of the mind through ceaseless practice of Guru Bhakti Yoga.

52. When the dissipated rays of the mind are collected by the practice of Guru Bhakti Yoga you can work wonders.

53. Guru Bhakti Yoga cult greatly stresses upon the service of Guru for attaining the purity of heart, to meditate and realise.

54. A true aspirant rejoices to the practice of Guru Bhakti Yoga.

55. First understand the philosophy of Guru Bhakti Yoga, then put into practice. You will succeed.

56. A very effective way of rooting out all evil qualities is to put into practice sincerely the Yoga of Guru Bhakti.

Fundamentals of Guru Bhakti Yoga

57. Absolute faith in the preceptor is the root of Guru Bhakti Yoga tree.

58. Ever-increasing devotion, humility, obedience, etc., are the branches of the tree. Service is the flower. Self-surrender to him is the immortal fruit.

146

59. You are bound to succeed in the practice of Guru Bhakti Yoga if you have a firm faith and devotion to the life-saving feet of Sadguru.

60. True and sincere surrender unto the Guru is the essence of Guru Bhakti Yoga.

61. Practice of Guru Bhakti Yoga means an intense pure love for Guru.

62. No progress in the Yoga of Guru Bhakti is possible without honesty.

63. Live in a quiet place with higher spiritual vibrations under a Guru who is a great Yogi or adept. Then practise under him the Yoga of Guru Bhakti. Only then you can attain success in the Guru Bhakti Yoga.

64. The ringing note of the Guru Bhakti Yoga is unconditioned self-surrender to the lotus-feet of Brahma Nishta Guru.

Cardinal Notes in Guru Bhakti Yoga

65. According to the Guru Bhakti Yoga school of thought Guru and God are one; hence, total self-surrender to Guru is very essential.

66. Self-surrender to Guru is indeed the highest rung in the ladder of Guru Bhakti Yoga.

67. Service of Guru is a *sine qua non* in the practice of Guru Bhakti Yoga.

68. Grace of Guru is the end or goal of Guru Bhakti Yoga.

69. Pig-headed student cannot have any definite progress in the practice of Guru Bhakti Yoga.

70. Evil company is an enemy of a disciple who wants to practise Guru Bhakti Yoga.

71. Give up sensual life if you want to practise the Yoga of Guru Bhakti.

72. Everyone who longs to transcend misery and obtain joy and happiness in life should sincerely practise Guru Bhakti Yoga.

73. True lasting happiness can be had by taking recourse to Guru Seva Yoga, but not in external perishable objects.

74. Is there no escape from the unceasing cycle of births and deaths, pleasure and pain, joy and misery? Listen, O disciple, there is one sure way, turn away your mind from the sensual objects which are perishable and take recourse to Guru Seva Yoga which takes you beyond dualities.

75. Real life begins when a man takes recourse to Yoga of Guru Bhakti which bestows on the practitioner the ever-lasting happiness here and hereafter.

76. Practice of Guru Bhakti Yoga gives you immeasurable and immense joy.

77. Guru Bhakti Yoga bestows on the practitioner longevity and bliss eternal.

78. The mind is at the root of Samsara or world process. The mind is the cause for bondage and freedom, pleasure and pain. This mind can be controlled only by practice of Guru Bhakti Yoga.

79. Guru Bhakti Yoga confers immortality, eternal bliss, freedom, perfection, perennial joy, and everlasting peace.

Greatness of Guru Bhakti Yoga

80. The avenue to the supreme peace begins from the practice of Guru Bhakti Yoga.

81. Whatever may be acquired by asceticism, renunciation, by other Yogas, by charity and auspicious acts, etc., all these are speedily acquired by practising Guru Bhakti Yoga.

82. Guru Bhakti Yoga is an exact science that teaches

the method of overcoming the lower nature and attaining the supreme bliss.

83. Some people think that Guru Seva Yoga is inferior type of Yoga. They have thoroughly misunderstood the secret of spirituality.

84. Guru Bhakti Yoga, Guru Seva Yoga, Guru Sarana Yoga, etc., are synonymous terms. They are one and the same.

85. Guru Bhakti Yoga is king among all Yogas.

86. Guru Bhakti Yoga is the easiest, surest, quickest, cheapest, safest way for God-consciousness. May you all attain God-consciousness in this very birth through the practice of Guru Bhakti Yoga.

Instructions to the Students

87. Take recourse to Guru Bhakti Yoga and regain your lost divinity.

88. Practise Guru Bhakti Yoga and go beyond all that causes duality and sorrow.

89. The practice of Guru Bhakti Yoga bestows on the disciple supreme peace, joy and immortality.

90. It is very easy to tame a wild tiger, lion or elephant. It is very easy to walk over the fire or water. But it is very difficult to surrender to the Lotus-Feet of Sadguru unless a person has real aspiration to practise Guru Bhakti Yoga.

91. Guru Bhakti Yoga is control of mind and its modifications through the service of Guru.

92. Perfect unconditioned self-surrender to Guru is the sure way to attain Guru Bhakti.

93. The foundation of Guru Bhakti Yoga is based on absolute faith in Guru.

94. If you really want God, turn away from worldly

enjoyments and take recourse to practice of Yoga of Guru Bhakti.

95. Continue the practice of Guru Bhakti Yoga without any interruption.

96. Practice of Guru Bhakti Yoga alone can make one fearless and ever happy in all walks of life.

97. Seek the immortal blissful Atman within through the practice of Guru Bhakti Yoga.

98. Make the Yoga of Guru Bhakti the only purpose, aim and real interest in life. You will reach supreme happiness.

SIVANANDA ADHYATMA SUTRAS

1. The way to God lies through the heart.

2. Religion is best expressed through ethics and morality.

3. Goodness is the price, happiness the reward.

4. Conquest of mind is the greatest victory.

5. God is one in all, and all in one.

6. To define God is to deny Him. But He is attainable through the practice of goodness, self-discipline, inquiry and meditation.

7. Example is better than precept. Silent example is better than loud example.

8. Thought determines character; character impels action; action decides the future.

9. Man, thou art a pilgrim here. This world is a vast university.

10. The goal is one, the paths are-many. The paths should not clash.

11. Superiority and inferiority complexes are products of ignorance.

12. Reformer, reform thyself first.

13. All work is sacred. Work is worship.

14. Evil cannot be destroyed, but practice of goodness will detract evil.

15. Truth is found in a peaceful, pure heart, which has freed itself from attachment and illusion.

16. If you want to find peace, be dispassionate and content.

17. Cowards can never realise God.

18. Let your life be a long prayer, dedicated to the service of God through the service of fellow-beings.

19. Gross self-interest is the root of all misery.

20. Solitude is in one's own heart.

21. Happiness is in detachment.

22. Fulfilment is emptying the heart of' all impurities and desires.

23. Expect nothing, and you shall know no disappointment.

24. Justice is found from one who thinks not of himself.

25. The path of righteousness is the guiding tract of duty.

26. God knows what is best for you. Do your duty as a trustee of the Divine, not as a proprietor.

27. Do not blame others. Everything is for your good.

28. A pure mind is your best friend.

29. Hate none, belittle none, hurt none. The same Lord dwells in all.

30. By injuring others you injure yourself.

31. Take care of your thoughts, your life will take care of itself.

32. It is a sin to be pleased with oneself. But by shutting out the possibility of progress, self-inquiry and introspection, the process of degeneration sets in.

33. No religion is superior or inferior. What is best for one, may not be good for another.

34. You do not want to be hated; therefore hate not others.

35. You do not want to be deceived; therefore deceive not others.

36. You do not want to be hurt; therefore hurt not others.

37. You do not want others to be angry with you; therefore be not angry with another.

38. You do not wish to be treated unjustly, therefore be just.

39. You do not wish others to have evil intentions towards you; therefore have good intention towards all.

40. 'Do as you wish to be done by' is not only a noble ideal but a practical necessity.

41. Do the right and be content and peaceful.

42. It is easier to pull down than build; therefore be positive, constructive.

43. Be charitable in mind and action, so that your heart may expand.

44. Charity of material goods is easier than charity of mind.

45. What comes from heart, goes to the heart.

46. Mind your own business and leave others to theirs.

47. No one is a fool always, and no one is wise at all times; therefore have respect for all and condemn none.

48. God is the end, the world the means. God is the target, the world the bow, and man the arrow.

49. One should profit himself by the world, and not become a bridled slave to it.

50. Love of fellow-beings means being helpful to others.

51. One cannot do selfless service and yet be self-centered.

52. Take care of today; tomorrow will take care of itself.

53. Grace of God flows equally towards all. Those who open their hearts to it, realise its presence.

54. Do not brood over the past and build no castles in the air. Live in the present.

55. Honesty, truthfulness and sincerity, patience, tolerance and simplicity, humility, nobility and forgiveness, love, compassion and courage, strength of will and mind, confidence, boldness and selflessness, — are the marks of Dharma.

56. Be not vain, arrogant, self-conceited. Close, and those shall be shut out. Open, and thou shall be filled.

57. Be wise like Nachiketas, virtuous like Yudhishthira. merciful like Buddha, devoted like Prahlada, determined like Bhima, dutiful like Rama, and pure like Jesus.

68. Purify, concentrate, reflect, meditate, realise.

59. Adapt, adjust, accommodate.

60. Be good, do good

SIVANANDA PRASNOTTARI

CHAPTER I

Q. Which is your arch enemy?

A. Egoism.

Q. Who is really beautiful?

A. Who is endowed with divine virtues, viz., courage, humility, tolerance, truth, cosmic love.

Q. Which leads to bondage?

A. Desire.

Q. What leads to freedom?

A. Desirelessness.

Q. What is real Karma?

A. Thinking.

Q. Who is a dunce?

A. He who identifies himself with the physical body.

Q. Who is a rich man?

A. He who has knowledge of Atman.

Q. Who is a beggar?

A. He who is full of desires.

Q. What is the horrible disease?

A. Birth and death.

Q. What is its remedy?

A. Brahma Jnana.

Q. Which is the worst fire?

A. Lust.

Q. What is real world?

A. Mind.

Q. Who is your real friend?

A. God.

Q. Who is a beast?

A. A passionate man.

Q. What are the worst intoxicants?

A. Wealth, power and lust.

CHAPTER II

Q. Where can you find eternal happiness?

A. In your own Atman within.

Q. Which is the most troublesome organ?

A. Tongue.

Q. Who is your terrible enemy?

A. Mind.

Q. Who is your best friend?

A. Satsanga or association with the wise.

Q. Who is your real father?

A. Guru.

Q. Which is the best language?

A. Language of the heart.

Q. Which is the best virtue?

A. Brahmacharya.

Q. Which is the worst intoxicant?

A. Lust.

Q. Which is the most sacred river?

A. Brahma Jnana.

Q. Who is the real king?

A. A Jivanmukta or liberated sage.

Q. Which is the best Dharma?

A. Selfless service.

Q. Which is the worst quality?

A. Anger.

Q. Which is the best thing in this world?

A. Pain (because it is the eye-opener, it goads you to seek liberation).

Q. Which is the best food?

A. Hearing of the Srutis or Upanishads.

Q. Who is the best man?

A. A kind-hearted man.

Q. Who is the worst man?

A. A selfish man.

Q. Where is the worst hell?

A. In the mind filled with jealousy, crookedness and hatred.

Q. Where is the best heaven?

A. In the heart filled with love, mercy and generosity.

Q. Which is the best silence?

A. Brahma Vidya or science of Atman.

Q. Which is the most precious thing in this world?

A. Vairagya or dispassion.

Q. Who is the strongest man?

A. He who practises Ahimsa, he who can bear insults, injuries and persecutions with smiling face.

Q. Who is a weak man?

A. An irritable man.

Q. Who is the most happy man?

A. A Tyagi or a man of renunciation.

Q. Who is the most miserable man?

A. A rich man.

Q. Who is the most beautiful man?

A. A Yogi.

Q. Who is the most ugly man?

A. A greedy man.

Q. Who is a beggar?

A. He who has desires.

Q. Which is the biggest ocean?

A. Ocean of Bliss (Brahman or Atman).

Q. Which is the most dangerous thing in this world?

A. Company of a worldly man.

Q. Which is the greatest temptation?

A. Woman for a man, man for woman.

Q. Which is the most desirable thing?

A. Brahma Jnana.

Q. Who is the best engine driver?

A. God.

Q. Which is the wonderful machine or engine?

A. Mind.

Q. Which is the biggest factory in this world?

A. Mental factory.

Q. Who is a real drunkard?

A. He who is intoxicated with the pride of wealth and learning.

Q. Who is a real blind man?

A. He who has no inner divine eye or the eye of intuition.

Q. Who is the real cobbler?

A. He who thinks that the body is Atman and talks always of matters concerning the body.

Q. What is your foremost duty.

A. To find out this hidden driver of this body-engine, to love Him, to live for Him, to serve Him, to know Him, to realise Him, to live in Him and to merge in Him.

CHAPTER III

Q. Who are the thieves?

A. Lust, anger and greed.

Q. Who is blind?

A. A lustful man.

Q. Who is a great man?

A. A sage who has knowledge of Atman.

Q. What is beneficial to man?

A. Satsanga (company of sages).

Q. Which is the best tonic?

A. Brahmacharya.

Q. Who is a weak man?

A. An irritable man.

Q. Who is a strong man?

A. He who can bear insult and injury.

Q. Which is the biggest sacred river?

A. The river of Jnana.

Q. What is more than death?

A. Dishonour.

Q. What is the most sacred Tirtha?

A. Satsanga.

Q. What makes one absolutely fearless?

A. Brahma Jnana.

Q. What is the best philosophy for one in this life on earth? Can you explain in simple words?

A. Be good, do good.